Delhi, in Thy Name

Adrija Roychowdhury is a journalist by profession and a historian by passion. She was born in Kolkata in 1990 and completed her graduation from Lady Shri Ram College in Delhi. After completing her master's from Delhi University and New York University, she has been writing for leading national dailies in India like the *Indian Express* and *Hindustan Times.* In her writing, she weaves contemporary socio-political events with deep historical narratives, archival research and voices of people. *Delhi, in Thy Name* is her first book.

Praise for the book

A brilliant portrayal of the people, bazaars, neighbourhoods, by-lanes and thoroughfares of a historic and ever-changing shahar. Roychowdhury converses with residents, digs into records, and she walks you through the streets of Delhi to reveal a city with a rich encrusted past. A must read.

—**Shahid Amin**, Retired Professor of History at Delhi University and author of *Conquest and Community: The Afterlife of Warrior Saint Ghazi Miyan*

In this lively, well-researched book, sparkling with insights, Adrija Roychowdhury reveals the many fascinating layers of history and memory connected with the names of Delhi's localities, bringing them alive through the voices of people who live there, giving us a new understanding of their depth of meaning. This is a valuable addition to writings on Delhi's present and past.

—**Upinder Singh**, Professor of History, Ashoka University and author of *Ancient Delhi*

Adrija Roychowdhury's evocative book takes us on a historical tour of Delhi through stories about its localities, their names, their recent pasts and memories of more remote origins. The histories of people and places unfold gently and beautifully, enabling the reader to grasp the complexities of the metropolis, with its several lives. And it makes us reflect on the processes of naming and renaming of places. A splendid work!

—**Amar Farooqui**, Professor of History at Delhi University/ Historian and author of *Zafar and the Raj: Anglo-Mughal Delhi c. 1800–1850*

In Adrija's free-wheeling record of her wanderings through Delhi neighbourhoods, their names are explained by the inhabitants in terms of their perceptions of a larger history. The author, to her credit, lets them speak for themselves. It leaves us with a sense of the fortitude with which this city has been built and survives. A promising first book.

—**Narayani Gupta**, Historian and author of *Delhi between Two Empires 1803–1931: Society, Government and Urban Growth*

Delhi, in Thy Name

The Many Legends That Make a City

ADRIJA ROYCHOWDHURY

RUPA

Published by
Rupa Publications India Pvt. Ltd 2021
7/16, Ansari Road, Daryaganj
New Delhi 110002

Sales centres:
Allahabad Bengaluru Chennai
Hyderabad Jaipur Kathmandu
Kolkata Mumbai

ISBN: 978-93-5520-039-6

Second impression 2022

10 9 8 7 6 5 4 3 2

Printed in India

Dedicated to my little world: Mona (my father), Ma, Bhai, Thamma, Didama and Snuffy

اگ رہا ہے درو دیوار سے سبزہ غالب
ہم بیاباں میں ہیں اور گھر میں بہار آئی ہے
उग रहा दर-ओ-दीवार पे सब्ज़ा ग़ालिब
हम बयाबां में हैं और घर में बहार आई है
DILAPIDATED WITH PLANTATION ARE THE
WALLS OF MY HOUSE GHALIB
THEY SAY WHAT A SCENE BUT FOR ME
IT'S NO MORE THAN A FOREST GLIB

Contents

Foreword

Delhi is not among the oldest cities in the world. Legend ties it to the Pandava's capital of Indraprastha, but the historical evidence of Indraprastha as a city and its location in Delhi is nebulous at best. Popular memory identifies the site in the village of Indarpat, which till a hundred years ago was located inside the Purana Qila, but archaeological excavations have revealed evidence of habitation from almost 2,500 years ago. Moreover, there is no evidence of any settlement with the complexity of a city in such ancient times, whether in the Purana Qila or elsewhere in Delhi.

The earliest evidence we have of a city named Delhi, or as it was then known, Dhilli, comes from the area of Mehrauli, around the Qutub Minar. Historians believe that the fortification which we today know as Lal Kot, was this city, founded by Anangpal Tomar II in the mid-eleventh century. Here too, there is a powerful legend that came to be associated with the history of the founding of the city. According to it, the city was founded by Anangpal at the site of a large iron nail that stood on the hood of the mythic serpent Vasuki. The iron nail in question is identified with the famous iron pillar of Mehrauli, a Gupta era artifact that still stands in the Qutub Minar complex.

The city may not be very old, but it is certainly of great historic importance. Founded as a frontier defensive town by the Tomars, Delhi rose to prominence under the Turks, who, coming into India via Afghanistan, conquered it during the late twelfth century. Soon after, it became the capital of an expanding empire, and since then, with some interregnums, it has been a capital; under successive Sultanate dynasties, under the Mughals during a large part of their rule, under the British from 1912 to 1947, and of Independent India.

The historic city of Delhi also has a peculiarity. The area of historic development has, for most part, been confined to the triangular area between the Yamuna River and the Aravalli mountains (known in Delhi as the Ridge); but several different sites within this area have been used at different times to build cities. These have numbered more than the proverbial seven cities—Lal Kot, Kilugarhi, Siri, Tughlaqabad, Jahanpanah, Firozabad, Din Panah/Shergarh, Shahjahanabad and New Delhi.

Another feature of Delhi, which it shares with other capitals of large, multi-cultural states, is the diversity of its population. This has long been the case. Even in ancient times, what later came to be Delhi, was on an important trade route, the Uttarapatha, which connected the Ganga Jamuna doab to territories in the north-west. This prominent location on a high road had prompted Emperor Ashoka to locate one of his rock edicts in Delhi, which can still be found in Kalkaji.

Delhi's position on an important trading route would have made sure that it was not insular in its culture, but it became truly cosmopolitan with the coming of the Sultanate. As the capital city it attracted immigrants from West and Central Asia as well as other parts of the Indian subcontinent. They came to Delhi in search of opportunities and made it their home. They brought with them their beliefs, languages and lifestyles, which added to the city's multicultural character.

While on the one hand Delhi became the home of many different communities, all retaining important aspects of their culture, there was also considerable mingling, which led to the creation of aspects of a shared culture. This was most evident in the field of language. The local Khari Boli was enriched with vocabulary from Persian, Arabic, Turki, in addition to words from other Indian languages, to create the language that we today know as Urdu. In the field of religious practice, the Sufi strand of Islam borrowed practices from the Indian traditions. This created an ethos centred on the many Sufi dargahs in the city, which attracted followers from different religions, and also contributed to other aspects of culture such as music. The association of music was particularly a feature of the dargah of Nizamuddin Auliya, a legacy of the saint's foremost disciple, Amir Khusro, who was also a renowned poet and musician.

The culture is often called Ganga Jamuni, after the rivers, the Ganga and the Jamuna. The two originate in different locations, then for a length flow parallel to but separate from each other, and for another part of their journey, their waters mingle in the same channel. The rich multiculturism as well as syncretism has long been a feature of Delhi's culture, and so it continues. The history of the city, rooted in its sites, but also carried in the memories of its people, continues to be made. Whether it is the legend of Indraprastha, or the founding myth of Dhillika—one lost in the mists of time, the other connected to surviving physical structures—both show us how popular belief and stories as well as historical evidence are used by people to understand the past of this great historic city. The same is the case with many other places and their histories, which are tied in the popular imagination with present imperatives and visions of the future.

This book looks at the city through the names that are associated with some of its neighbourhoods, old and not so old. In the process, it not only goes into the question of the origins of place names, and the politics of naming and renaming, but also engages with popular memory. Historical research combined with journalistic field work makes this a unique contribution to the vast literature on Delhi.

The many shifts in the meaning of 'Chandni Chowk' are unpacked, from the founding of the main market square by the princess Jahanara in Shahjahan's Delhi, to what people now understand the word to mean. The difference is not just between the past and the present, but also between what residents understand and how visitors label the area. In this 'Old Delhi', the name we often give to seventeenth century Shahjahanabad, many names and stories are lost or imperfectly remembered, and Adrija explores these through interviews with residents and historians. Also unpacked are the layers in the name Connaught Place—its origins, its persistence despite official renaming and a rare interview with the originator of the renaming—Mani Shankar Aiyer.

Despite its antiquity, the rapid expansion of Delhi as the metropolis we know came after Independence. New neighbourhoods were created, and with that came the process, often emotionally and politically charged, of naming. What were the alternatives that were considered to 'Chittaranjan Park' as the name for a colony of settlers from East Bengal? What are the histories of Kashmiri migration to Delhi that are enshrined in Pamposh Enclave? What connection does Ayodhya, which is also called Saket, have with Delhi? How did Shaheen Bagh, a name today associated in the popular mind with a political movement, grow out of and beyond Jamia Nagar, named after the university that was founded as a result of another political movement a hundred years ago? These are some of the questions that the author sets out to explore and answer, and takes us on her journey of discovery.

Swapna Liddle
Historian and author

Introduction

In October 2018, a piece of news coming in from Uttar Pradesh had left many divided over the implications it might have. Heated debates had ensued on social media; historians and political scientists were consulted to decode the development in the state which had, just about a year back, brought the Bharatiya Janata Party (BJP) to power in a sweeping majority. This was neither a bloody riot, an accusation of scheming corruption, lynching or harassment of the minorities, nor was a statue being erected in the name of boosting tourism.

Rather, it was a simple and harmless change of nomenclature—Allahabad was now Prayagraj. Following the state government's decision, a minister is believed to have declared valiantly, 'Today the BJP government has rectified the mistake made by Akbar.'[1] Soon after, public emotions drew a sharp line of division between those who felt that the name change had finally undone centuries of 'historical wrong', and those who were mournful about the slice of history that was lost in the process.

I have never visited Allahabad and hence, cannot claim to have any personal sentiment attached to its name. Neither had I, before this particular development, reflected upon the alleged 'historical wrong' that the name Allahabad possibly contained within itself. But I had, in fact, frequently mused over the almost musical quality of the name.

'Allah-a-abad' or rather 'illahabas', as the Mughal emperor Akbar sought to name it in the sixteenth century, is the 'place where holiness dwells.' The sanctity of its soil had for generations attracted Hindu pilgrims who basked in the united sacredness of the Ganga, the Yamuna and the mythical Saraswati. The Mughals, enamoured by the godliness associated with the area, wished to urbanize it and thereby, gave it its name. The British too were attracted to the character of Allahabad and saw it to be of importance in terms of military strategy. Thereby, the city was made the capital of the United Provinces.

Allahabad was home to the Nehru-Gandhi family. It also produced iconic leaders of the Rashtriya Swayamsevak Sangh (RSS), the BJP and the Vishva Hindu Parishad like Rajendra Singh, Murli Manohar Joshi and Ashok Singhal respectively. The city gave birth to leading scientists like Meghnad Saha and Daulat Singh Kothari and literary giants like Firaq Gorakhpuri and Harivansh Rai Bachchan. The third-century Ashokan pillar existing in the city is evidence of its link with a Buddhist past, while the Allahabad fort standing right next to it, is testimony to the city's development among the Mughals.

Journalists Shyamlal Yadav and Seema Chisti described most evocatively the roots of cultural amalgamation in Allahabad in a column in the *Indian Express*: 'Sitting at the confluence of the Ganga and Yamuna (and the mythical Saraswati), Allahabad may well be seen as the birthplace of North India's celebrated Ganga-Jamuni sanskriti, the symbolic reference to the coexistence of many cultures in a harmonious blend, much like the two mighty rivers that meet here.'[2]

Why then was its name being considered a 'mistake'?

The change in nomenclature was justified on the grounds that the point at which the three Hindu religious rivers met was known as 'Prayagraj', and that the Mughal ruler Akbar had conquered the place, built his city on it, giving it the name 'Illahabas', which was later anglicized as Allahabad. The explanation was on the same lines which has, for years, characterized the Hindu Right's reading of Indian history—Muslim rule on Hindu soil was a mistake. The argument, of course, left no space for reflection upon the historical development of a place, carrying within itself the multiple moods and characters with which it identified itself at different points in time. For sure, Prayagraj might very well have existed as a Hindu pilgrimage site for much longer. It was Allahabad though, which gave the city its distinctive character and everything iconic that it went on to produce, including the very special '*Allahabadi surkha*' (A much loved, special variety of guava cultivated across Allahabad).

Surely, the name change decision cannot take away from Allahabad all that it is and has produced over time. Why then, was there a furore over a decision as innocuous as the renaming of the city? What is it that the name of a city, a place, a street or an institution carries within itself?

Delhi, in Thy Name is an attempt to answer this question. This book is a close scrutiny of the naming of the streets and neighbourhoods in the capital of the country. It is a reflection upon the politics, emotions, aspirations, desires, identities and of course the undertones of seemingly innocent decisions that go into the naming of a space. Most importantly though, the book is a response to the socio-political times in India at present.

Allahabad is one among the many cases of name change that have characterized India since the 2014 general elections, when the BJP came to power in the centre with a pathbreaking majority. In May 2015, Aurangzeb Road in Delhi was renamed after the former president of the country, A.P.J. Abdul Kalam. In April 2016, Gurgaon in Haryana became Gurugram after Guru Dronacharya who appeared in the Hindu epic Mahabharata and the historic Mughal Sarai railway station in Uttar Pradesh was rechristened after the RSS ideologue, Deendayal Upadhyaya. More recently, Faizabad district in Uttar Pradesh was renamed as Ayodhya (believed to be the birthplace of Lord Ram), and in September 2019 after the demise of the BJP leader Arun Jaitley, Feroz Shah Kotla stadium came to be renamed after the leader. Himachal Pradesh's Shimla has been considered to be renamed as Shyamala, while a suggestion was made to rename Hyderabad as Bhagyanagar but was later refuted.

This is not to say that the practice of name change is a new development in the last seven years. The pages of history are replete with moments of revolutions and regime changes—moments when entire dynasties have been toppled, those when individuals have taken centre stage and of course, those when the marginalized have risen to assert their own identities. Bloodshed and newer forms of governance are typical of these moments, and the change in street names, were just the harmless accompaniments through which memories and spaces were reimagined. For that matter, there are sufficient examples of historical moments world over when entire landscapes were redrawn with newer names.

The historical trajectory of France is an interesting case in point here. In 1755, a 19-acre octagon was constructed between Champs-Élysées to the west and the Tuileries Garden to the east and it was named the Place Louis XV, to honour the then ruler of the country. The place had a grand equestrian statue of the King as well. About three decades later, when the French Revolution took place, the statue was torn down and the place was renamed 'Place de la Revolution'. Soon after, the revolutionaries placed a guillotine on the site and the King was executed there. The site which was once constructed to honour the French throne turned into the symbol of its downfall, with several figures of French royalty being executed there. In the ensuing years, the name of the octagon has changed on several occasions, symbolizing the political mood of the time. In its present form, it got its name 'Place de la Concorde', first in 1795 and later in 1830, as a symbol of post-revolution reconciliation.

With the establishment of the Third Republic in 1870, innumerable streets and squares in Paris were renamed. In his tourist guide to Paris written in 1882, the English author Charles Dickens describes most aptly the pattern of naming streets in the French capital:

> It is worth observing that in the French nomenclature, the French authorities avoid calling two streets by the same name... Names of every sort and kind are chosen: the names of capital towns, of great statesmen, of generals, of authors, of musicians, of sculptors, of painters etc. It is easy enough to find new names for streets; and by so perpetuating the memory of a man who has deserved well of his country, the wanderer in Paris does not in his day's peregrinations come across eleven Queen streets, a dozen King streets and Duke streets without number, which as we all know, happens in London only too frequently.[3]

While the difference in the patterns of nomenclature between Paris and London would make all too evident the variegated nature of the two country's political histories, Dickens is quick to point out that 'the frequent changing of the names of their streets is not to be commended; and under the present Republic the practice seems to have been pushed to an unusual extent. But this love of alteration has long been common in Paris.'

One can perhaps safely say that the rampant change of street names in Paris is a mark of a historical trajectory of the country, which has changed its course all too frequently.

But not always do we find regime changes being accompanied by a change in the names that it had guaranteed. The occurrence of historical episodes and the preservation of its memory may very well not go hand in hand. Take for instance, the case of Russia, wherein, the Russian Revolution had heralded a spree of name changes that firstly did away with memories of the Tsarist regime and secondly carried within it everything that the new Soviet regime represented, including its leaders, philosophers, moments of victory and pride, as well as terminologies representing its ethos.[4]

The change in street names which accompanied the downfall of the Soviet government in 1991, was, however, far more complicated. The name of Joseph Stalin for instance, had been erased out of the Soviet Union long before 1991. By the end of 1993, about 153 street names had been changed in Russia, out of which 102 had a clear link with the Soviet past.[5] But then the name of the founder of the Soviet government, Vladamir Lenin, continues to adorn thousands of streets and neighbourhoods in Russia. In 2015, the Russian web mapping service, *Yandex.maps* identified more than 5,000 streets in Russia bearing the name 'Lenin', while more than 6,500 streets carried the name 'Soviet' in them.[6] The name of 'Leningrad', however, was changed back to its original 'Saint Petersburg' after the collapse of the Communist regime.[7]

Germany is yet another case in point, where street names have been studied minutely to understand the dynamics and symbols of political changes in the country. The naming of the Rosa-Luxemburg-Platz at Berlin is an interesting study in this regard. The square gained reputation for being the site at which the Communist Party of Germany opened its headquarters in 1926, and it continues to house the headquarters of the German Left Party. The square was named 'Bülowplatz' in the pre-Nazi period. With the establishment of Nazi rule, the square was renamed as 'Horst-Wessel-Platz', after the Nazi party leader Horst Wessel, who was murdered in 1930 and was remembered as a Nazi martyr. After the fall of the Nazis in 1945, the square was renamed yet again, first after the German communist Karl Liebknecht, and then later after the Polish social revolutionary, and communist leader Rosa Luxemburg.[8] The current name of the place is a reflection of the dominant communist ideology in post-war East Berlin.

When it comes to India, after the British left the

country, names of many cities and states were changed to reflect local linguistic and phonetic preferences. Cawnpur, for instance, was changed to Kanpur in 1948. Jubbolpore became Jabalpur. In the 1990s, Bombay became Mumbai, Cochin was changed to Kochi and Calcutta was renamed as Kolkata. As recent as April 2020, the government of Tamil Nadu changed the names of as many as 1,018 places so that they are pronounced in the way the local population of the state does.[9] Consequently, Coimbatore was changed to 'Koyampuththoor', and Vellore became 'Veeloor'.

Politics of renaming essentially boils down to erasing a past that one does not wish to be associated with and imposing one that is most at ease with the ideology of a governing party. In the post-Independence era for instance, streets carrying names of British officials were renamed by the Congress government to reflect Indian nationalist or cultural icons. Curzon Road in New Delhi was renamed as Kasturba Gandhi Marg after the political activist and wife of Mahatma Gandhi. Similarly, Kitchener Road was renamed as Sardar Patel Marg.

The recent wave of name changes by a ruling party well known for its Hindu nationalist ideology, is a similar attempt to erase the memory of a Muslim past in India. The objective also is to impose a name that clearly reflects the 'correction' of supposed 'historical wrongs' that a party in power wishes to reiterate. In August 2020, for instance, a day before the Ram temple bhoomi pujan in Ayodhya, former union minister and member of the ruling BJP, defaced the Babur Road signboard in Central Delhi. He demanded that the road now be called '5 August Marg' instead, after the date on which the Ram Mandir bhoomi pujan would be held. As his rationale, Goel held up what is undoubtedly the fiercest debate in modern Indian history which the ruling party had recently laid to rest: 'Babar was an invader who attacked Hindustan and demolished Ram Mandir. The PM is going to perform a ground-breaking ceremony for a grand temple in Ayodhya tomorrow. At such a time, it will be an appropriate move to rename Babar Road as 5 August Marg.'[10]

But it is important to note, that not all acts of renaming are imposed by those in authority. Many a time, the demand for a change of a particular place's name comes from its people. An interesting case here is that of a small village in Austria which recently changed its name to Fugging from its previous name, 'Fucking', which in colloquial English translates to an act of sexual intercourse.[11] Reports on the name change in international press noted how the residents of the village were tired of the 'mockery' that they were facing because of the name. English-speaking tourists would frequently click pictures besides the signposts at the entrance of the village to post on social media. In the last few years, about a dozen or so such signposts of the village have been stolen. The village was named after a Bavarian aristocrat called 'Focko' who founded the settlement in the sixth century. The residents of

'Fucking' were so embarrassed of the name, that they did not mind wiping off the history of its origins along with the name.

Similar instances are found in India as well. Residents of a hamlet in Bihar named 'Pakistan' have been petitioning the local government to change its name as it has become a point of anxiety for them. The villagers say that they do not wish to be identified as Pakistanis, given that they have nothing to do with the country. Reports on the petition carry comments from village residents lamenting the fact that no one wishes to marry their daughters because of their village's name and that the worsening relations between India and Pakistan is affecting their relationship with the neighbouring villages.[12] Ironically, there are no Muslims in this village and is largely dominated by a tribal population. It came to be named so in memory of its Muslim residents who migrated to East Pakistan (now Bangladesh) in 1947. The Muslim residents had handed over their property to the Hindus who stayed back in the village and in return, they named the village 'Pakistan'. Today though, this little history of love and coexistence is something that the villagers would rather be rid of. Instead, they wish to name their village, 'Birsa Nagar' after the renowned tribal leader Birsa Munda.

A 2016 report in the *Hindustan Times* noted that in the last three years, thirty villages from across India have applied for a name change. Among them is the village 'Beef' in Uttarakhand. The majority Hindu residents of the village wanted the name changed since it went against their religious beliefs. Consequently, in 2014, the village was renamed as 'Narayanpuri'. Then there was Chorachi-Wadi in Satara district of Maharashtra, which in Marathi means, 'a place of thieves'. In 2014, the Home Ministry allowed it to be renamed as Anandpur. More recently, residents of a village named 'Korauna' in Uttar Pradesh have been demanding its name to be changed. The residents say that ever since the coronavirus pandemic became global news, they are constantly ridiculed and face discrimination.[13]

It is important to note though, that not all requests for name changes are met with success. The process is complicated and time consuming, and the Union Home Ministry does not allow for a new identity of a village unless the reasons are absolutely pressing.[14] However, some requests are indeed accepted. This was the case with the village 'Ganda'. In 2016, twelve-year-old Harpreet Kaur had written a letter to Prime Minister Narendra Modi requesting the village's name to be changed. The Prime Minister, in turn, had taken personal interest in the matter, and had directed the authorities to approve the name change of 'Ganda' village. Consequently, in 2017, the Haryana government gave a nod to change its name to 'Ajit Nagar' after the eldest son of Sikh master Guru Gobind Singh.[15]

The same is not the case with Amar Singh Brar of Kuttabarh, also in Haryana. For the last 10 years, Brar has been writing petitions to various levels of the government, including the office of the chief minister for changing the name of his village, which in Hindi loosely translates to a space meant for dogs. However, he is yet to meet with success.[16] In essence, it all boils down to whether the popular demand for naming or renaming manages to incite political interest.

A common criticism against the act of renaming is that it deprives people of a sense of history. In 2015, for instance, Aurangzeb Road in New Delhi was renamed as A.P.J. Abdul Kalam Road. The idea was to wipe out the name of a 'cruel Mughal ruler' and replace it with that of one of the most popular president of independent India. However, what got wiped out in the process was also the way in which Aurangzeb Road came to be named so by the British. The British government, while making New Delhi, had strategically named roads after powerful Mughal rulers to reflect a sense of Delhi's history and find legitimacy for their own rule alongside that of the Mughals.

Both the act of naming Aurangzeb Road and renaming it were products of intense political processes which need to be documented as part of history. Street names, in that sense carry plenty of information, which provide important clues to the larger historical context in which they take birth. In a country like India, so variegated in its religious, linguistic, ethnic and cultural fabric, street names are a rich repository of identity politics, memories and overlapping histories. From extolling deities in the oversized Hindu pantheon, to introducing linguistic terms from countries near and far, from venerating heroes of imperialism, to those who lost their blood in the process of giving birth to a new India, from names of protagonists in popular epics, to those glorifying the aesthetics of the natural landscape of a region, from local anecdotes that find a safe place in the memories of a set of people, to grand historical episodes, place names in India are too diverse to be able to fit into the pages of a single book of analysis.

My efforts, therefore, are restricted to studying the toponyms of the national capital. Delhi is far from being representative of the moods, emotions and aspirations that make India what it is. Yet, a close look at the city's place names can serve as a point of entry into a world where names dominate everything that a region's populace looks up to, desires or had at some point in time desired. My attempt here is not to produce an exhaustive account of the names of places scattered across the city. Rather, it is simply to spark an interest into thinking of what the act of naming and renaming truly entails.

There is a popular legend about the founding of Delhi by a 'pious, brave and generous king' named Dilu or Dhilu, after whom the city came to be named. The seventeenth-century Persian chronicler in the Mughal court, Muhammad Kasim Ferishta is believed to have recounted the legend of Dilu and how he was, in the 40th year of his reign on the city, taken prisoner by Phur, the governor of Kumaon.[17] Like Dilu, the name of King Dilipa is also associated with the founding and naming of Delhi.

These stories of how Delhi came to be, have passed down through generations, and have been analysed by historians at various instances. Unfortunately though, there is very little sound historical basis to suggest who Dilu or Dilipa was, and indeed when and how did he build this city.

Delhi, known to be the city of eight cities, boasts of a legacy of political leadership of the kind very few other cities in the country can. Since the first millennium CE when the Tomara Rajputs took over its administration, it has been renamed on multiple occasions. While Qila Rai Pithora was named after the twelfth century Chahamana king Prithviraj Chauhan, Tughlaqabad was named after the fourteenth century Tughlaq monarch Ghiausuddin Tughlaq. Feroz Shah Kotla was named after yet another Tughlaq ruler who built his capital on the soils of Delhi, and then the Mughal Emperor Shah Jahan's Shahjahanabad gave the city its most recent name before being taken over by the British who preferred to call the capital 'New Delhi'.

It is interesting that despite the multiple names that have been enshrined over the capital at different points in time, it is the name from folklore, rather than sound historical evidence, which found popular acceptance among people and made its way to the administrative naming of the city.

My interest in studying the names of streets and neighbourhoods in Delhi stems from this unique element of surprise that the city and its people have to offer. I was not born in Delhi and neither did I encounter much of it while growing up in Jamshedpur and Kolkata, apart from being aware of the capital status it enjoyed. Rather, I was among the thousands who make this city their home each year, as they set foot in it in search of higher education. As an outsider, I have often been amazed at the myriad of stories or histories that one encounters at every nook and corner of this city.

An eighteenth century gurudwara, Majnu ka Tilla, built to commemorate an Iranian Sufi mystic, has over the years given its name to a colony providing shelter to Tibetan refugees. Partition refugee enclaves glorifying names of nationalist heroes of the likes of Lala Lajpat Rai, Madan Mohan Malviya, have amidst them colonies venerating regional cultural symbols. While names of majority colonial figures have been erased from the stones and pillars of the city, that which is enshrined upon the prime commercial complex of Delhi, Connaught Place, has strangely been favoured by popular consensus, despite attempts to rename it with names of icons of post-Independence India. The 'hauz', 'sarais', 'baghs,' 'chowks', lay comfortably alongside the 'avenues', 'streets', 'place', reminding the world of the overlapping epochs that have found peace in sharing a home in Delhi.

My story of Delhi's toponyms begins with Chandni Chowk, a 1.5-kilometre piece of road that stretches out from Red Fort to Fatehpuri Masjid. Designed by Shah Jahan's daughter, Jahanara Begum, Chandni Chowk was the central and most exotic market square in Shahjahanabad—the capital constructed by her father. The Yamuna ran down this street in all its elegance, and the square pool at which it collected in the middle of the street is believed to have glimmered magnificently in the moonlight, giving it the name 'Chandni Chowk'.

In the course of the next centuries, the entire street came to acquire the name 'Chandni Chowk' and in more modern times, all of Shahjahanabad came to be loosely referred to by the name.

It is worth remembering that even when 'Shahjahanabad' was gradually erased out of the old Mughal capital, the names of the countless lanes, bylanes, gullies, 'kuchas' and 'mohallas' remained intact. Names like 'Churiwalan', 'Katra neel', 'Roshanpura', 'Suiwalan', 'Matia Mahal', have been retained as it is since the days of Shah Jahan. In the collective identification of the entire area by the name 'Chandni Chowk', lies a more subtle story of the transformation in recent decades of Old Delhi, or the Delhi envisioned by its Mughal rulers.

When the British shifted its centre of power from Calcutta to Delhi in 1911, the idea was to appropriate the historical legacy of a city that had for centuries served as the capital for preceding dynasties. The British did not just shift headquarters, but also imagined a new city with the names of European imperial authorities written alongside Indian monarchs.

The new capital came up on Raisina Hill, on the site which was until then occupied by villages lying on the suburbs of Shahjahanabad. At the heart of it was Kingsway, a ceremonial boulevard dramatically sweeping down from the viceroy's house all the way to the sixteenth-century fort, Purana Qila. It was named in honour of King George V who announced the shift of the capital in the durbar of 1911. This road was bisected by another one which went by the name 'Queen's Way'. Those roads carrying the houses of the higher echelons of the government were named after the British monarch, like King Edward Road, Queen Victoria Road and King George's Avenue.[18] Then there were streets named after those who had a special role to play in the establishment and governance of the British Empire in India like, Clive Road, (named after Robert Clive), Hastings Road (named after Warren Hastings), Curzon Road and many others. Alongside these, were streets named after erstwhile Indian rulers. Roads named after Mauryan Emperor Ashoka, the Chahamana King Prithviraj Chauhan, Mughal rulers Akbar, Shah Jahan and Aurangzeb, were planned by the British typically with the objective of placing their own imperial ambitions in the same lines and space occupied by the high and mighty of Indian history.[19]

My second chapter is focused on the name of the circular market occupying the heart of Delhi—Connaught Place. Originally designed by the British for the European and rich Indian clientele of the new capital, it was named after a rather insignificant member of the crown, Prince Arthur, the Duke of Connaught, who was the uncle of King George V. The duke's contribution in the pages of Indian history is, in fact, quite limited, and yet his unflinching popularity among the people of Delhi in the form of a most beloved market right in the centre of the city is rather interesting to examine.

In the aftermath of the Independence of the country, there exist countless examples of streets and neighbourhoods where names of British rulers and officials stand erased and replaced by those believed to be sons of the soil. King Edward Road, for instance, was turned into Maulana Azad Road and Queen Victoria Road was renamed as Dr Rajendra Prasad Road. Yet the Duke of Connaught, despite his rather mediocre or almost absent record in the history of India, has been victorious in fighting the forces of name changes. In the 1990s, the Congress government had, in fact, attempted replacing his name with that of assassinated former prime minister, Rajiv Gandhi, but support for the British scion stood unwavering in the face of the descendant of a most powerful Indian political family.

The story of Connaught Place is a most interesting battle between the history of a country as its government would like its people to remember, and that which the people have chosen through free will to be part of popular memory. But it is also an account of Indian political history of the 1990s, and a reflection upon why the name of the leader of a most popular political party of the country stood rejected by the people of Delhi.

The British-built New Delhi gave way to a newer one soon after the Independence of the country. As the tricolour bid a final goodbye to imperial forces in 1947, and a blood-soaked Partition tore apart the subcontinent along religious lines, Delhi, continued to be the seat of power, but its contours were re-imagined yet again. The rapid growth in the population of the city reflected in the newer colonies being drawn out upon urbanized villages and in the spirit of nationalism still fresh in the minds of the new residents, they preserved their histories in Lajpat Nagar, Malviya Nagar, Tilak Nagar.

Dotted among these new colonies were also those where residents firmly grasped on to the heroes and cultural symbols that served as a reminder to the home they had left behind in the process of finding a safe corner in the capital of new India. What Chittaranjan Park was for the Bengalis, Pamposh Enclave was for the Kashmiri Pandits. What Hemkunt Colony was for the Sikhs, Punjabi Bagh was for the refugees of West Punjab.

My third chapter studies the naming of CR Park. The Bengali residents of this neighbourhood are the ones who had lost land and property in what became East Pakistan. Chittaranjan Das, or CR Das, who gives this

Bengali neighbourhood its name, was one of the many heroes of the nationalist movement from Bengal. The story of CR Park is really an account of the discussions and debates that the residents of this colony were engaging over what it was that best represented their post-Partition identity. But was Chittaranjan Park really their choice, or one that the government in power wished upon them? The naming of CR Park holds clues as to why large parts of post-Independence Delhi is marked by names of freedom fighters.

Right opposite CR Park is Pamposh Enclave which forms the subject for my fourth chapter. It is a neighbourhood built to house the Kashmiri Pandit migrants in Delhi. The colony derives its name from the Kashmiri word for lotus, *pamposh*. Wrapped up in the name are the memories of a home left behind in Kashmir, the aspirations to build a newer one in Delhi, and also the multitude of grievances that have plagued the Kashmiri Pandit community for decades.

Gradually mushrooming alongside the migrant and refugee community neighbourhoods were those which housed the aspirational, upwardly mobile, who visioned a lush future in Vasant Vihar, Green Park, Panchsheel Park.[20]

As the ideals of secularism remained ingrained and celebrated in the constitutional structure of the country and in the speeches of its leaders, a fairly quiet spirit of 'Hindu nationalism' expressed itself in residential colonies like Saket, Greater Kailash and Janakpuri.

In my fifth chapter, I examine the story of Saket, a name which, to a Delhi resident, successfully conjures up images of everything modern and ambitious, including glamorous malls and broad boulevards. Hidden beneath it though, is a silent acceptance of Hindu mythology to represent a neighbourhood largely dotted with ignored remnants of medieval Indian Islamic history. Saket, as many would know, is another name of Ayodhya, believed to be the birthplace of Lord Ram. Interestingly though, Saket is the name that is frequently used to describe Ayodhya in Buddhist literature.[21]

While on one hand, colonies were expressing consciously or subconsciously majoritarian sentiments, on the other hand, were those which glorified minority identities and preserved them in the likes of Jamia Nagar and Ambedkar Nagar.

One such neighbourhood, Shaheen Bagh, has in recent times grown to acquire international fame as the face of minority identity and aspirations in the country. Its name, derived from a poem written by Muhammad Iqbal, forms the subject of my sixth chapter. *Shaheen,* meaning falcon in Persian, was a word popularized by Iqbal in the years preceding the Independence of the country. He used it extensively in his poems to inspire the Muslim community in India. The choice of the word in representing this little colony in Southeast Delhi is intriguing in terms of the unique cultural and political identity that Muslims in post-Partition India chose to represent themselves.

I could go on for pages commenting upon the thousands of names sprawled across Delhi. But for the purpose of this book, I have focused my attention upon these six neighbourhoods of Delhi, each with a distinct character, and a unique historical trajectory of its own. This is by no means an academic discourse on the history of names in Delhi. Rather, as a journalist, I have tried to keep these six neighbourhoods alive by placing the focus on its people.

It is through the people of Delhi, their lived experience and their little anecdotes, which clearly did not make their way to the history textbooks, that I tell the story of the names in Delhi.

Chandni Chowk

A shadow of shimmering moonlight over
Shah Jahan's beloved city

WALLED CITY WELCOMES YOU
CHANDNI CHOWK
चांदनी चौक
چاندنی چوک

'Chandni' translates as moonlight and 'chowk' is a square. My tryst with this square drenched in moonlight began in the final year of college when our professor of Mughal history, in an attempt to enliven a rather bored group of students, decided to introduce us to the 'exotic' lanes of Chandni Chowk through references to interesting anecdotes about the havelis (palatial houses) that continue to dot its landscape. He patiently discussed Chunnamal Haveli, Zeenat Mahal, Begum Samru's palace among several others, and to many of us who had spent much of our lives outside Delhi, the description of the magnificent havelis was a thrilling experience. We made up our minds that we had to visit this moonlit square and explore the exquisite havelis.

So, on a pleasant winter morning my friend Namrata and I set out in a quest to rediscover Chandni Chowk. We decided to take the metro to the station that went by the same name and hoped to be magically transported to a whole other historical era when we stepped out. Much to our disappointment, far from glowing with Mughal exoticism, the chaotic electric lines sketched across the skies was all that was most striking about the place. Of course, the waves of human crowd that mercilessly pushed us around was something we had not expected from the moonlit square of our imagination. But the most confusing part was the fact that there was no square at all, and the havelis were more often than not, tucked away most inconspicuously in between shops and restaurants.

As we roamed aimlessly, we encountered a Delhi very different from the plush south where we lived, but still a far cry from what we had hoped to witness. By the time we decided to call it a day, we were exhausted from having strolled around a large number of streets, corridors and neighbourhoods, but had no idea as to where we could find that moonlit square. Neither did we know where Chandni Chowk began and where it ended.

Over the years, I have visited Chandni Chowk on several occasions, sometimes in pursuit of the unique variety of food it has to offer and at other times to proudly reflect upon the rich history of a city I had eventually grown to make my own. But the perimeters of Chandni Chowk continued to be a bit of an enigma to me. I might not be completely wrong in suggesting that Chandni Chowk is almost an idea, an ambiguous space where one can find the best paranthas, jalebis, kebabs, wedding garments and jewellery in Delhi.

Modern Delhi's understanding of Chandni Chowk is rather vague. Those who live in and around the area would tell you that the name refers to nothing else except that one road which stretches out from the Lahori Gate of the Red Fort and ends near the Fatehpuri Masjid.

Yet, for those who live far away from the area, Chandni Chowk is loosely used to refer to large sections of what happens to be the city that Shah Jahan had built back in the seventeenth century. So much so that even an attempt to map Chandni Chowk on Google will give one the same result. Interestingly, while most people are aware of the Mughal monarch's contribution to that part of the city, it is very rare for his name to come up in conversations mapping out a civilization that Shah Jahan had envisioned to be his own.

In order to understand what Chandni Chowk was or is, we need to reflect upon the way it was conceived, designed, built and altered over time. Its story goes back to the seventeenth century when Shah Jahan was the emperor occupying the Mughal throne and had dreamt of creating a city that would reverberate in the glory of his name.

By 1639, the Mughal Emperor Shah Jahan had already been ruling from Agra for more than ten years. A connoisseur of architectural delights, Shah Jahan is known to have spent much of his time in planning the design and establishment of different administrative and non-administrative buildings across the length and breadth of the city. Historians note that the emperor spent some amount of time every day at the Diwan-i-khas, discussing various plans of governance with his ministers. 'An important order of business during these meetings was the examination of designs of buildings which were laid before him by the architects and superintendents of construction.'[1]

By the late 1630s though, the emperor no longer considered Agra to be an ideal site from which he could rule. The capital city that Shah Jahan had inherited from his father lay on the banks of the Jamuna and had over the years undergone severe erosion. 'The main gate of the palace-fortress had become too small for the crowds that gathered on court days and festivals, and many persons had been bruised or crushed as they tried to squeeze inside.'[2] He now wanted to create a new city, one upon which his name would be etched in gold for posterity to gloat over. The Mughal historian Inayat Khan who has chronicled the life of Shah Jahan in his work, *Shahjahannama,* noted that 'the thought came to his mind that he should select some pleasant site on the banks of the river, distinguished by its genial climate, where he might found a splendid fort and delightful edifices.' He further noted that 'streams of water should be made to flow through the proposed fort and that its terraces should overlook the river.'[3]

For a brief moment Lahore was considered for the new project. But Lahore was considered too crowded and unattractive.[4] Finally Delhi was considered to be the ideal place for his purpose. By the mid-seventeenth century, the region had already served as capital city on multiple occasions in the past 500 years, first by Hindu rulers and then under Muslim rule. Even though Delhi stopped enjoying the status of a capital city about 150 years before Shah Jahan decided to place the crown on it yet again, the place was still noted to be of prime importance among Muslims in India. As historian Stephen Blake notes in his work, when an Englishman visited the court of Jahangir in 1609, he described Delhi to be the 'chief city or seat royal of the kings of India.'[5]

Delhi was also an important centre of religiosity for both Muslims and Hindus by then. After all, it contained the shrines of prominent Sufi saints like Qutubuddin Bakhtiyar Kaki, Nizamuddin Auliya and Nasiruddin Chiragh Dehlavi. The place was equally revered in Hindu mythological traditions. In vedic doctrine, Delhi was Indraprastha, the place where Lord Indra performed sacrifices and worshipped Vishnu.[6]

The Mughals were well aware of the political stature that Delhi held and the religious sentiments it could arouse among large segments of North Indian population. Accordingly, Shah Jahan prepared to design his new city keeping in mind both Hindu and Islamic architectural philosophies. The street plan was devised as per a semi-elliptical design suggested by a fourth-century text on Vaastu Shastra called *Manasara*.[7] This design, called the *karamuka* or bow, was considered most preferable for a site fronting a river or seashore and played an integral role in the way Shah Jahan's architects planned the city. In 1639, Shah Jahan's household astrologer drew out the most auspicious date for laying the foundation stone of the new city. Ceremonial sacrifices were carried out and religious rites observed as the Mughal Emperor declared the founding of his new capital—Shahjahanabad (the city of Shah Jahan).

If one were to view Shahjahanabad from the top, the only thing visible would perhaps be a closely knit mishmash of lanes and corridors. Chaos is the most defining aspect of Shah Jahan's city. There is absolutely no set pattern in the way streets cut into each other or seamlessly open out into new ones. Scholars of urban planning have frequently remarked upon the chaotic structure of 'Islamic' cities. These same people have also been criticized severely for their lack of vision in setting bars of organized planning based on what they observed in the European world. In my opinion though, the disorganized street plans in this erstwhile Mughal city is symptomatic of a world that was democratic, living with a free spirit that allowed neighbourhoods, market spaces, streets and cul-de-sacs to develop as and how it was most convenient for its residents.

Over the centuries, what remains of Shahjahanabad has grown to be more disorderly with elements of modernity like tangled electric wires, piles of construction material and roads dug up for fitting pipelines, adding to its already confused landscape. So closely does the place identify with chaos that one would not be surprised to find a Lutyens' Delhi resident twitching his nose at the very mention of it and maintaining distance from it, unless the occasional need of 'exotic' food or wedding garments arises.

Modern Delhi's most remarkable achievement,

the metro, has of course made things easier, making the travel between the newer parts of Delhi and Shah Jahan's city an affair that takes less than an hour to complete. The metro in fact has been instrumental in bringing together the past and present of the city. When I decided upon decoding the mystery behind the naming of Chandni Chowk, it was the metro that came to my rescue, frequently transporting me back and forth from Chittaranjan Park (South Delhi's Bengali hub), where I was living at that moment. Those familiar with the geography of Old Delhi would agree with me that the moment one steps out of the Jama Masjid metro station, the sudden change of character of Delhi is unmistakable.

The whiff of kebabs and biryani in the air, the smattering of Urdu in the language of the people, the skull caps and burqas that dominate its streets, easily distinguish this part of the city from the rest of Delhi. But the vendors selling piles of saffron and yellow rice, and skewers filled to their very tips with chunks of meat are the first ones to greet you. Ask them if their biriyani contains beef or buff and they nervously shuffle their feet as they hesitantly respond with a soft yes. The street they are lined up on, stretches out from the front of the Jama Masjid (the central mosque commissioned by Shah Jahan) and is known as Meena Bazaar. Apart from the food delights, the street is also lined up with vendors selling scarves, burqas and caps, among several other things. As I got chatting with one of the biryani vendors,

I asked him if he knew why this street was called the Meena Bazaar. 'You should do research and find out,' he responded curtly, disappointed in not being able to answer my question. 'This market has been there since the time of the *badshahs* (princes), how would I know why they named it so?'

I could not find the reasoning behind the naming of the street from anyone in Meena Bazaar. It was only after I came back home and did some research into its origins that I realized, Meena Bazaar was not named after something or someone. Rather it was a concept in itself that is part of large sections of the Muslim world. During the Mughal rule, Meena Bazaars were typically markets that would be put up exclusively for women. The name perhaps caught on to the imagination of the people and several cities that have experienced long periods of contact with the Islamic world consist of a Meena Bazaar, or occasionally set up such spaces.

For that matter, the concept of a bazaar in itself has intimate connections with the Islamic world. Scholar of Islamic architecture, Mohammad Gharipour, has put together a richly detailed book *The Bazaar in the Islamic City: Design, Culture and History,* in which he writes that 'the bazaar has played a key role in the economic, cultural and even political transformation of cities throughout the Islamic world. Such a central role has made it an integral part of the city, often the generator of urban form and the definer of urban elements.' In other words, the bazaar in the Islamic world is significant in the way in which a city develops. Unsurprisingly, throughout the crisscrossed network of Shah Jahan's city, the 'bazaar' either in its name or in its concept is something that one comes across most frequently. Either these are markets selling specialized products and are named after them, or they are the kinds that put on sale an assortment of objects for everyday use.

The Meena Bazaar ends in front of the Jama Masjid's steps and as one climbs up and looks towards the city on the left, it is yet another bazaar that greets you. The Urdu Bazaar as it continues to be called has a distinct scholastic texture to it. There are several bookstores or what is locally known as 'kutub khana' that line up the street. I entered one of them and met Ali Khusrou, a short, lean gentleman in his seventies or eighties. Ali has been the manager of the bookstore since the 1970s. He gave me a brief insight into the history of the street. 'Urdu Bazaar has been situated here for centuries. We know that during the time of Shah Jahan when people would come here from across the world to offer prayers or for trade, they would visit this place for buying books.' Ali explained that the business in Urdu books began during that period and this entire street was lined up with such stores. Today only about fifteen Urdu bookstores remain on the street. When I asked if the sale in Urdu books has reduced over time, Ali denied, firmly shaking his head. 'Urdu is a *muqammal* (complete) and *khubsoorat* (beautiful) tongue,' he said in a language so beautiful that it could never be captured on paper. 'It is not possible for you to say anything without some amount of Urdu.'

It is worth noting that under the Mughal rulers, Persian and not Urdu was the language of the court. The elite spoke in Persian, while Urdu was born and raised among the commoners. For that matter, the language actually came into existence back during the time when Delhi was ruled by the Sultanate. It was developed in the army garrisons when soldiers who spoke Persian mixed with those who spoke Hindavi. For a long time, it remained a mere dialect, before its popularity peaked and it came to be considered as a literary tongue. Under the Mughals, Urdu had grown to flourish. Though it was still not a court language, its popularity among writers of literary works was well established. Today it is considered to be the de facto language of the Muslim communities in this part of the world, while for others it continues to be a language that one longs to hear, speak and experience.

The naming and placement of these two bazaars, is in fact an interesting example of the way in which memories of the names of historical spaces are retained in newer geographies. A women's market or Meena Bazaar was held inside the Red Fort during the Mughal rule.[8] The Urdu Bazaar was originally placed in the space between the Lahore Gate of the fort and first square on the street running down right in front of it. It got its name from being so close to the square in front of the fort where the army was stationed.[9] Both the bazaars disappeared after the British destroyed large parts of the old city following the revolt of 1857. Evidently, the British were successful in erasing these markets from their physical landscape but not from the hearts of the people of Delhi. With time a new Meena Bazaar and Urdu Bazaar came up in the vicinity of the Jama Masjid.

As I walked down beside the multiple bookstores that line up Urdu Bazaar, I reached the turn that led to what is perhaps the most popular street in that part of Old Delhi today. This is Matia Mahal, the street that consists of some of the most iconic restaurants of the city including Karim's, Al-Jawahar, Aslam and several others. My interactions with the residents and vendors on this street made me realize that the history behind the naming of this street is rather obscure. Every person I spoke to, had a different story to tell. A bright, young, enthusiastic boy, Moinuddin, cut into my conversation with one of the other vendors to excitedly tell me what he knew about the naming of Matia Mahal. 'I have heard from my elders that in old times this street was lined up with mud (matti in Hindi) houses. Hence the name Matia Mahal,' explained Moinuddin. An owner of a restaurant that specializes in Biryani, Moinuddin was quick to advertise his product before I could leave. 'Once you have tasted my biryani, no other biryani across the world will be able to satisfy you,' he declared valiantly.

Food is the most conspicuous product on this street. It is hard to walk even two steps without being called out by some vendor who is trying hard for you to try their kebabs, nehari, rabri or shahi tukda. It was by chance that I happened to enter the restaurant owned by Mohammad Jahangir. Jahangir was the first and only person in my entire research tour within Shah Jahan's city who referred to the area as Shahjahanabad. 'This area is called Jama Masjid, Shahjahanabad, market Matia Mahal. Now no one calls it Shahjahanabad anymore and it is simply called Matia Mahal.' Jahangir provided me with an explanation on the naming of Matia Mahal that was remarkably different from the one given by Moinuddin. 'Matia Mahal is named after a haveli (palatial house) of one of Shah Jahan's princesses. Now the haveli has been broken down and turned into a school,' he said. Indeed a few metres away from Jahangir's restaurant does stand a school, but it is hard to tell historically if it was once a haveli wherein one of Shah Jahan's princesses lived.

Nonetheless, Jahangir's stories had my heart and I spent a good one hour listening to him with rapt attention. He took great pride in the nihari cooked in his restaurant and narrated to me in great detail how the dish came into existence when Shah Jahan was imprisoned by his son. Another object very dear to him is a sketch of Jama Masjid that has been passed on for generations in his family. Apparently, it shows Jama Masjid when it was first built and also depicts the monarch visiting it with elephants, horses and soldiers on either side. When I pleaded with him to show me the sketch, he smiled knowingly and asked me to come on another day. 'You can see it, but cannot photograph it,' he cautioned. According to Jahangir, his ancestors worked as builders in Shah Jahan's court and were in fact involved in the construction of the Jama Masjid. Later they were given plots of land in the newly constructed city to build their residences in. 'We had our shops on the ground floor and our homes above them,' he explained. Jahangir evidently basked in the glory of his Mughal past. Right when I was about to leave, he enthusiastically invited me over to watch the pigeon race he conducts each year on Republic Day.

Matia Mahal seamlessly leads one to a y-shaped street that goes by the name 'bazaar chitli qabar'. One of the boys who has a flower shop situated right at the juncture where the road forks out, told me that the street derived its name from a mausoleum (qabar) that is located right behind his shop. 'So, who is buried there?' I asked rather intrigued. The boy shrugged his shoulders to denote that he had no idea. I immediately walked off to take a look at this mystery mausoleum that gave the street its name. After walking for about half a kilometre I could not find anything. By this time people around me were quite amused by the lost look on my face and asked me what I was looking for, more out of pity than anything else, I believe.

When I told them that I was trying to locate the Chitli Qabar they immediately directed me back to the beginning of the street which I had crossed few minutes back. I was confused since there was absolutely nothing I had seen there. It is only when one of the men walked me to the actual spot that I finally encountered a tiny grilled room that had a grave inside. The room was locked from outside and it was only through the narrow gap in between the grills that I could see the grave. It was so dark and obscure that I am still surprised as to how such an unnoticeable structure could give an entire street its name.

As I was trying hard to get some view of the mausoleum, the man who had walked me to it suddenly called out to a young boy resting on his bike a few steps away. His name was Fakhru Malik and he owned a shop selling perfumery products on that road. A lean short boy in his twenties, dressed in a yellow t-shirt and a pair of ripped, blue jeans, Fakhru told me that he had grown up beside the mausoleum. He explained in great detail how he has seen families coming there for generations to pay respect to the man buried in the grave.

'This grave has a history that goes back 800 years, even before the Jama Masjid was built,' he explained with much conviction. 'This entire road was filled with graves,' he said, right after which the other man whispered something in his ears. 'He is saying that even today there are homes in this street that contain old graves that have not been demolished,' said Fakhru.

When asked about who is buried in the grave, Fakhru said that he was not sure but there are many people who have a lot of faith in this gentleman and firmly believe that their despairs will come to an end if they pay respect to him. 'His followers come here frequently and they are the ones who take care of this mausoleum and clean it up occasionally,' he said.

I have never really given much thought to what Shahjahanabad was before Shah Jahan made it his capital city. Hardly do the large network of streets and lanes within it tell anything of a past that existed there before the Mughals made it their home. Bazaar Chitli Qabar, in that sense, was an exceptional encounter. It is interesting to note that the mausoleum's existence has been coupled up with 'bazaar' to give it a distinct urban flavour, characteristic of the Mughal city.

An off shoot of Bazaar Chitli Qabar is a street that goes by the name Suiwalan. The shopkeepers on the street, most of whom sell meat or kebabs, explained to me that during the Mughal era this street specialized in the sale of needles (sui), and that is how it got its name. At present though, there is not a single trace of this trade in needles that once supposedly flourished here.

Leading out of suiwalan is another interesting road that goes by the name Gali Takhat Wali. The street is largely a residential neighbourhood. On asking around a bit, the residents explained to me that *takhat* means a wooden bed in Urdu. One such bed was placed right at the end of the street and that is what gave the neighbourhood its name. I was wide eyed when I heard this—a little bed can give an entire street its name? Of course, I had to take a look at this historic takhat.

Excitedly I walked to the end of the street where I was met with two plump looking elderly gentlemen sitting on a dust-covered wooden platform. When I eagerly asked them where the takhat was, they were amused. 'We are sitting on it,' they said in unison.

I am not sure if my disappointment was visible or not, but I continued probing further with the expectation of some interesting anecdote to come my way. 'This takhat is famous all over Hindustan,' said Abdul Razak and Abdul Ghani who were sitting on it. 'In earlier times elderly gentlemen sat here and took care of small, local issues of dispute among residents. It would almost be like a panchayat. Nowadays people generally sit here and drink tea or read the newspaper,' explained Razak. 'Can women sit on it?' I asked almost knowing the answer to my question. I was not at all surprised when they said no. When asked about how long back into the past this takhat was placed there he quickly responded—'During the time of the badshahs (Mughal kings)'.

The Mughal past seems to be embedded within the lanes, by-lanes and the very psyche of the people who live in this part of Old Delhi. Hardly ever did I come across a conversation in which the words 'badshahs', 'Mughal' or 'Shah Jahan' did not feature. It was almost as if the Mughal past was living and breathing in this part of the city. It definitely did give a lot of matter for the residents of the area to gloat over.

I would have wanted to walk in further to encounter more such names and stories that made Shahjahanabad.

However, it was time to take a look at a different part of the city. So, I carefully made my way back to Urdu Bazaar, all the while hoping not to lose my path in the massive labyrinth of streets and stories that I was leaving behind.

The part of Shahjahanabad that I had been exploring is known to be dominated by a Muslim population. It was time to visit the other part that is largely inhabited by Hindus and Jains. Whether or not it was always the case is hard to tell, but at present this is the way the demographic of this area is divided. The best way to understand the division would be to keep the Jama Masjid as the focal point and find Hindu and Muslims on either side of it. In order for me to reach the Hindu neighbourhoods I would have to go around the mosque. But the local residents insisted that the fastest way would be to go through the Jama Masjid and step out from gate number three of the mosque.

From the very moment that one steps out of gate number three of the Jama Masjid, Shah Jahan's city suddenly changes its personality. Gone are the kebab and biryani stalls. They are replaced by piles of thick, greasy jalebis, crispy samosas and kachoris. The language of the people also undergoes a significant change. The smattering of Urdu, characteristic of that part of the town gives way to Hindi. But this is not Hindavi or Hindustani, as was the case for a long time before the Partition changed demographics of Old Delhi. The Hindi spoken on the streets now is of a very different kind, with a notable amount of contribution from Punjabi.

Chaos though, is as characteristic of this part of Old Delhi, as it is on the other side of Jama Masjid. But it is no longer just the physical landscape that is chaotic. The confusion spreads further into the way people identify the place they are living in. As I walked straight from the Jama Masjid, I was rather surprised to note how shops located right beside each other often identified themselves with different addresses. For instance, 1441, Bazaar Guliyan, Dariba Kalan, Jama Masjid, Delhi-6, lies right beside 1442, Bazaar Guliyan, Jama Masjid, Delhi-6. Interestingly, the Jama Masjid Road that stretches out from right outside Gate 3 of Jama Masjid is suddenly referred to as Pai Walan by some of the shops that stand on it.

A bearded gentleman with a skull cap was a rare sight to come across on this side of the town. He was idling beside one of the shops on the Jama Masjid Road or Pai Walan. When I asked him about the reasoning behind the name, he explained to me that *pai* means foot. Now the naming of the road could be the product of two things. First, perhaps the place was occupied by traders who sold the foot of beds over. Alternatively, it is also possible that the street earlier consisted of vendors selling legs of lambs, goats or beef. Now neither of the two businesses are alive on the street. 'After the Partition, all the shops selling meat have shut down, since this is now predominantly a Hindu locality. Meat shops are all on the other side,' he said with a smile.

As one keeps walking down Jama Masjid Road, it leads on to the Esplanade Road. It is interesting to come across this name here. It carries within it echoes of a Victorian past when the concept of an esplanade had come up to denote a large open space typically lying next to a water body. It is a name that one quickly associates with the British rule in India, particularly in the cities they considered most fit for trade because of the presence of water bodies in them. Interestingly, there is an Esplanade Road in Kolkata, Mumbai and Chennai, all three cities where the British established their presidencies. Of course, we know that Shahjahanabad was changed in significant ways after the British encounter with the rebels of 1857, but largely the names of the streets had not undergone much transformation. Hence a road by this name in this part of the city is in fact an exceptional case.

But there is also something to be said of the precise location of this street and its link with the wreckage of the city by the British following the revolt. In the immediate aftermath of the suppression of the revolt, the British decided that large parts of Shahjahanabad had to be destroyed for security purposes. This included getting rid fortifications, walls, and several buildings both within and outside the fort. An area of five hundred yards in width of shooting distance around the fort was what was decided upon to be cleared out. Eventually, they stopped short of four hundred and fifty yards.[10]

Esplanade Road was the name given to the street that ran almost like a boundary land between the part that was cleared out and the point at which old settlement began. Thereby, while an esplanade would normally lie on the edge of a settlement against a waterbody, in the case of Shahjahanabad it lay on edge of settlement against empty land.

But the naming of Esplanade Road also has a large amount of confusion within it. One of the shop owners on the road told me that it is also called the Ramchandra Dehlvi Marg. Dehlvi was a noted leader of the Arya Samaj, who is known to have spread knowledge on the vedas among scholars in Old Delhi. Yet again, the occurrence of his name on the streets of Shahjahanabad is suggestive of the way names and historical episodes have overlapped in this part of the city. It is worth noting that this same road is also often referred to as 'old cycle market', in indication of the cycle trade that was historically a part of this street and continues to be so to a small extent.

Walking around the nooks and corners of this part of the erstwhile Mughal city, one gets the feeling of two pasts competing to make space for themselves. It is hard to tell which historical epoch will confidently take centre-stage here.

The Jama Masjid Road shoots out to a small neighbourhood called 'Gali Guliyan'. A quick look around will tell you that it is the favourite lane of brass idol makers in Delhi. Exquisite idols of Krishna,

Ganesh and every other Hindu Gods is present here and so are a large range of metal antiques. One such brass idol-maker, Vinod, welcomed us to the locality with the anticipation that I might be interested in his products. As I got into an intense conversation with him on the history of this neighbourhood, he explained to me that 'Gali Guliyan' translates as *Gali goliyon ki.* In other words, it is the lane of gun shots. 'When the country was divided, there was a lot of gun firing in this area.' A swift recce of the neighbourhood would make it clear that it is a predominantly Hindu locality, which again as Vinod explained, is a product of population exchanges made during the Partition when the Muslims left the area and the Hindus took it over.

But if the name 'Gali Guliyan' is a product of the Partition, then clearly it had to be named something else earlier. By this time Vinod along with his fellow shop owners had gotten into a fierce debate on who was to be blamed for the Partition. I could hear angry references to Jawaharlal Nehru when I interrupted to ask what the street's name was before the Partition. 'Of course, this market was there before Partition as well,' said Vinod. He immediately pointed to an old, ignored, dilapidated structure which he said was the *Diwan khana* or a district court during the Mughal era. The district court of Shah Jahan's time is now visible only in ruins, and so is the past of Gali Guliyan which is now discernible only through the little anecdotes that the residents have to share.

As per local beliefs, the architects who designed the Red Fort, Hamid and Hira, had been given large properties in this area and that there existed two *mohallas* (neighbourhoods) named after both of them there. Interestingly, the name of Hira here seems to be a product of popular imagination, since it's a well known fact that the Red Fort was designed by Ustad Hamid and Ustad Ahmad Lahauri. If local anecdotes were one set of sources that told me about the story of Hamid and Hira, then the other was a tiny blind alley that was hidden somewhere within Gali Guliyan. It was named as 'Kucha Hira'. Kucha Ustad Hamid, also located close by, retains the name of the other architect. Kucha translates as a cul-de-sac.

Ustad Ahmad Lahauri's name, however, finds no mention in the many streets of Shahjahanabad. It is worth noting that street names at the time when the old city came up, had less to do with commemoration and more to do with popular landmarks. Kucha Ustad Hamid was named so, not in honour of the architect, but because his estate lay along that street. Same is the case with Hira, whose name has been conjured up in popular imagination as being one of the master architects. Perhaps Ustad Ahmad Lahauri did not have a home or property in the area, which explains why his name finds no mention in the dynamic display of street names here.

By the time I left the small remnant of Shah Jahan's architects' past, one thing was clear to me. We know that the naming of a locality involves the creation of a certain historical trajectory. What also accompanies it is the destruction of a different past which in the popular memory of the inhabitants might just be of lesser importance given the circumstances. Hamid and Hira were important actors in the history of Gali Guliyan. Important enough for people to recollect their existence, just not important enough to continue offering their names to the area that had once achieved its reputation because of their being.

A few kilometres away from Gali Guliyan, and yet again an off shoot of the Jama Masjid Road, is one of the most popular markets in this area that goes by the name Dariba Kalan. When I first came across Dariba Kalan a few weeks back, my travel companion Rachna Dixit had excitedly explained to me that the name is derived from the Persian—*Dur-e-be-bahan* that translates as 'pearl beyond compare'. The name, as it would appear, was an ode to the numerous jewellery shops that line up this street. Residents and shop owners though, seem to disagree with Rachna's understanding of the meaning of Dariba Kalan.

One of the most conspicuous shops on this street is one selling a wide variety of perfumes. It's owners, who have been in the business for the last two hundred years, told me that it's the first shop of its kind in this area. One of the shop managers, Rupal, was busy attending to his customers when I approached him and was visibly disturbed by my relentless probing into the history of Dariba Kalan. A semi-bald man of medium built, wearing a crisp white cotton shirt and grey trousers, Rupal had a soft and urgent way of speaking. His shop was remarkably different from his average office-going attire. Glass containers of different shapes and sizes, filled with liquids of exotic red, blue, green, dotted every corner of this room. The floor was covered with a maroon carpet, while Rupal sat on a *divan* (a couch like sitting furniture), on one end of the room.

'The literal translation of Dariba Kalan would be, Dariba as in market and Kalan as in big,' he explained once he realized that I refused to leave without getting some dose of historical anecdotes from him. But once he started speaking, Rupal went into a rant about the Mughal past of the area. It was almost as if he could visualize the royal dynasty come alive in front of him. 'This entire street would be covered by a shade. Mughals would go through here from Red Fort to Jama Masjid for trade.' Rupal went on to explain that the adjoining lane which is now referred to as 'Kinari Bazaar' was earlier called 'Dariba Khurd'—'Khurd' means small. Earlier both these markets would sell a large number of articles for everyday use. 'With the passage of time, the occupations of the people here have changed and so have the names given to these places. Dariba Kalan is now Sarafa which means jewellery and Dariba Khurd is Kinari Bazaar owing to the trade in fabric borders that takes place there. Over time of course, Kinari Bazaar has also become the street that sells all kinds of wedding garments.'

Branching out of Dariba Kalan is a dark, narrow alley that goes by the name 'Lattu Shah ki gali'. It is hard to tell who Lattu Shah was, but residents of the place will tell you that he was a dear friend of Shah Jahan, almost like his brother. No historical source actually mentions a friend of Shah Jahan by that name. The renowned chronicler of Delhi, R.V. Smith noted that this street was named after a saint associated with lattus or spinning tops, but no one knows why.[11] But then again, local historical anecdotes often have a life of their own. Lattu Shah may or may not have existed, but his name did give the inhabitants of a little lane a few moments of pride in being associated with the Mughal throne.

I was strolling in Dariba Kalan and around it when I happened to land onto the street that has over the years been made hugely popular by television and cinema. I had first heard of the 'Paranthe wali gali' at a television reality show wherein the participants were competing over who could devour the maximum number of paranthas. Back then I was not a resident of Delhi and the idea of an entire street being named after paranthas had come across as rather amusing to me.

The L-shaped corridor actually has only four shops specializing in paranthas. The rest of the street is largely occupied by shops selling wedding garments and ornaments. But that was clearly not the case in the past when this entire street consisted of vendors selling hot greasy paranthas and lassi. The origins of this specialized food business is attributed to a certain Babu Ram, whose family owns the four shops on the street. The shops claim to date themselves back to 1889, when Babu Ram had first opened his shop here. The great grandson of Babu Ram, Ashish, who was managing one of the shops that day, explained to me that Babu Ram had come to Delhi from Bhind in Madhya Pradesh in the nineteenth century. The story goes that he was a wrestler inside the Red Fort and once he had saved enough money through his wrestling career, he decided to invest it in a parantha shop here. Eventually, as his business prospered, those around him also opened similar shops, so much so, that this little street at one point boasted of 18 parantha shops. Over time though, with rapid commercialization of this space, most have switched businesses or have moved out of the neighbourhood.

I exited the 'Paranthe wali Gali' to reach the one road that most non-residents of Old Delhi use to loosely refer to almost any and every part of this region. The Chandni Chowk is a long, broad road that begins at the Lahori Gate of the Red Fort and ends in front of the Fatehpuri Masjid. At that time, large parts of the street lay dug up for the sake of the redevelopment work being carried out by the Delhi government. But I do not remember a single occasion when I was visiting this street and did not find it crowded to a degree that one need not even walk. It was inevitable to be pushed around and gasp for breath, even while the desperate garment sellers on the street are calling out to try their latest collection of lehengas (a richly embroidered skirt like garment, mainly worn during wedding and other traditional functions). The commercial nature of this street is unmistakable. Shops selling food, clothes, electric appliances, exotic varieties of lamps and lights and several other commodities line up the street. Also evident is the way different time periods have comfortably adjusted themselves here, living beside each other with ease. If on one side of the road we have the famous *jalebi wala* whose family is believed to have set up the shop back in the nineteenth century, then on the other side modernity makes its presence visible in the form of a McDonalds outlet.

It is also interesting to note how a Jain temple, a Shiva temple, a gurudwara and a church are present together on this same street. Residents and shop owners in this area will tell you that during the rule of the Mughals, the Yamuna flowed down this street in all its glory, shimmering in the reflection of the moonlight above. It pooled into a large square somewhere in the middle of the road and the reflection of the moon here was breathtakingly beautiful. This square was surrounded on all sides by shops, cafes, caravanserai and a bath house or what was known as the *hammam.* It was actually an important public square where people would sit down to enjoy a leisurely day. It was in fact just this octagonal square that was originally named as 'Chandni Chowk'.

Chandni Chowk was conceived by Shah Jahan's daughter Jahanara Begum. The most beloved of her father, Jahanara was an extraordinary woman, both ambitious and accomplished. She is known to have invested her wealth in building large parts of Shahjahanabad. But Chandni Chowk was her pet project, one in which she had wrapped all her dreams. It is impossible to reflect upon the legacy and popularity of this street without hearing about the power and ambition held by its patron and what all she hoped to achieve through the busy moonlit square.

In 1648 the entire Mughal household including Shah Jahan's ministers and amirs moved into the completed palace-fortress in Delhi. Jahanara Begum, the eldest and the most loved daughter of the emperor was thirty-four years old then and possibly the richest and the most powerful woman in the Mughal Empire. Legend has it, that when she stepped out of the fort she would be followed by cavalry, infantry, slow-moving elephants and Abyssinian eunuchs who would announce her arrival to the walled city with much pomp and show.[12] By thirty-four, Jahanara, popularly known as Begum Sahiba, already commanded over the entire revenue from the territory and port of Surat and the revenue from the estate at Panipat.[13] 'She also owned the villages of Achchol, Farjahara, Safapur, Doraha, Medina and

Panipat.'[14] Upon her mother's death in 1631, Jahanara inherited property worth approximately five million rupees.[15] Apart from this, her father endowed upon her the largest allowance, leaving a meagre amount for his other children.

When the Italian traveller and writer Niccoli Manucci visited the Mughal court, astounded by the love and respect bestowed upon the Emperor's eldest daughter, he wrote 'she was loved by all and lived-in state and magnificence.'[16] The French physician and traveller Francois Bernier, on the other hand, described the affection and popularity enjoyed by Jahanara from her father in far more lascivious ways. 'It would be unjust to deny the king the privilege of gathering fruit from the tree he had himself planted,'[17] he wrote explaining the unnatural attachment.

By the age of thirty-four she was not only rich and respected but was also the most erudite in the Mughal household. Having attained a large amount of knowledge in the Chisthiya faith, she had already written two Sufi treatises. With the enormous amount of wealth at her disposal, she turned towards her father's new dream capital. Five of the nineteen imperial buildings had been commissioned by her and so was the market Chandni Chowk.[18]

This octagonal-shaped bazaar was in fact her dream project, one that would glow in her ferocious ambition for centuries to come. She commissioned it with much love and care and it was no tribute to her father or brother. It was all hers, telling the world of the power and reputation she held in the Mughal order of things.[19]

Shops selling all kinds of things came up around this square, making it one of the busiest markets. These shops occupied small rooms under arcades and were partitioned by thin walls. Author Ira Mukhoty, vividly imagined the scene at the central market in her book: 'There were traders from Turkey, Zanzibar, Syria, Yemen, Arabia, Iraq, Khurasan, China and Tibet besides Europeans from England and Holland. The goods sold there included rubies from Badakshan, pearls from Oman and fresh fruits from Kashmir and Central Asia. There were also weapons, fine cloth, perfumes, elephants, horses, camels, birds, water pipes and delicate sweets.'[20]

Jahanara's dreams for the central marketplace does not end there. To the north of the market, she built a caravanserai.[21] She is famously remembered to have remarked aloud once, 'I will build a *sarai,* large and fine like no other in Hindustan'. So it stood there as one of the most unique inns that welcomed travellers from around the globe. To the south, she made a garden and a hammam (public bath).

When Jahanara dreamt of the central marketplace in Shahjahanabad, there was no name that she pinned upon it. People simply referred to it as the bazaar in the direction of Lahore.[22] Sections of the street upon which it was placed though, had been named according to the trade or activity most popularly associated with it. For instance, the section of the street between the Lahori Gate of the fort and the chowk at the *kotwali chabutra* (police station) was called the Urdu Bazaar and it served the soldiers, servants and artisans of the imperial household. A different section of the road was called Ashrafi (moneychangers) or Jauhari Bazaar (jewellers' market) and was the financial sector.[23]

The Yamuna flowed gracefully down the middle of the street, watering a row of trees on either side. It came together in a large pool at the centre of the octagon built by Jahanara. On most days it reflected the light of the moon most perfectly. Soon people referred to the pool and the square as Chandni Chowk or moonlit square, as a tribute to the beauty of the moonlight. Eventually, the beautiful moonlight gave its name to the entire road from the Lahori Gate of the fort to Fatehpuri Masjid. It came to be called Chandni Chowk, displacing every other name on it.

It is hard to tell exactly when and how the name Chandni Chowk was transferred from the central public square to the entire street. It appears to have happened almost organically. If one were to believe the Persian writer Dargah Quli Khan who wrote the much-spoken-about book *Muraqqa-e-Dehli*, right before the city was attacked by Nadir Shah, then we would know that by the early decades of the eighteenth century, Chandni Chowk had already established itself as the principal marketplace in Shahjahanabad.

In the decades and centuries following the attack

by Nadir Shah, the city underwent remarkable changes both in its character and in its name. By the early nineteenth century, the city was turned into one of the territories of the English East India Company, though in word of mouth it was believed to be under Mughal rule. The British presence in the city was accompanied by a gradual erasure of the name 'Shahjahanabad'. Perhaps the word was too much of a tongue twister for the foreigners. It is also possible that the British wished to downplay the role of the Mughals by casually wiping away the name of the monarch who gave birth to the city. Whatever be the case, the British definitely did prefer referring to the city as Delhi rather than Shahjahanabad.

The revolt of 1857 further convinced the British that it was time to wipe away the Mughal character of the city. While they retained the names of the large number of galis and mohallas within the city, they did act upon its overall landscape. While the army was forced to barge into the fort and demolish a number of palaces, replacing them with barracks, outside in the city, several shops, havelis, public buildings and mosques were destroyed. Jahanara's beloved caravanserai was demolished and the premises of the Lawrence Institute was built in its place in 1860, named after John Lawrence, the Lieutenant Governor of Punjab province.[24] It consisted of the Chamber of Commerce, a literary society and a museum. In 1866 it was bought over by the municipality and turned into the Town Hall as it continues to exist today. As far as Chandni Chowk was concerned, the public square that gave the street its name was demolished, thereby removing the most iconic memory of Jahanara Begum's creation from the street.

*

By the early twentieth century the British realized that they needed to make further alterations in their administrative capacities. With the growing fervour of nationalism in Calcutta, it was considered necessary to shift capital to Delhi. But it was not the Delhi of Shah Jahan that they wished to recycle. The new capital of the British had to be close enough to the Mughal capital so as to symbolically lay claims to its historicity, while at the same time, not exactly on the same site so that it appears to be in every way their own. After much discussion and debate, the site of the new capital was chosen in the south of Shahjahanabad, at Raisina Hills. This was to become New Delhi and Shah Jahan's city received a newer name. Henceforth it was referred to as Old Delhi, as what it is still frequently called.

But the erstwhile Mughal city saw yet another wave of historical changes when the British left the country amidst large scale riots caused by the Partition. The demographics of Old Delhi underwent a significant change in the course of the violence and bloodbath of the Partition. While thousands of Muslims left the city for Pakistan, carrying with them their unique language, culture and traditions, they were immediately replaced by the Hindus from the other side of the border who had left behind their properties, lives, dreams and everything else. The identity and character of Old Delhi underwent a gradual change from this period on. While the change was most palpable in the demographics and the manners of its people, in its name too, somehow from then on, the entire area was loosely referred to as Chandni Chowk. This was definitely the case in popular culture and in the imagination of those who lived outside the premises of the walled city. Moreover, when modern Delhi was mapping out its electoral constituencies, this area was once again brought under the umbrella name of Chandni Chowk.

Shah Jahan's name was being gradually wiped away since the days of the British rule. But Chandni Chowk's pre-eminence also meant that it had overtaken the multiple little histories that had gone into the making of Shahjahanabad. In order to understand this transition, I knocked on the door of historian Swapna Liddle. Liddle is well known as one of the finest experts on the history of Delhi in India. Days before I approached her, she had released her latest book *Connaught Place and the Making of New Delhi*, and was at that moment actively promoting it on social media by luring her readers through small historical anecdotes from her book. Previously, she had written two exquisite books on Chandni Chowk and Old Delhi and had also been aggressively raising awareness on the heritage of Delhi.

I visited Swapna at her home in Maharani Bagh (a neighbourhood in Southeast Delhi) and over a cup of hot masala tea we got chatting on the naming and renaming of Shahjahanabad. 'How did the transition between Chandni Chowk as the name of the public square to that of the entire area happen?' I asked Swapna right away. 'Look at the way the Chandni Chowk metro station has been named. It was not always Chandni Chowk. They wanted to name it Old Delhi metro station. The traders' association wanted it to be called Chandni Chowk since it has become such a big brand name. That is how it happens. Once a name becomes so popular, even people who are slightly away want to be considered as belonging to that place,' she explained.

'But how did this transition happen historically?' I asked probing further. Swapna immediately went across the room to get hold of her laptop and pulled out two old maps for me. 'Look at this. This is a map of Delhi in 1857–58. Here, only this one public square is called Chandni Chowk,' she said pointing to a little square on the road leading out of Red Fort which was marked as Chandni Chowk. 'This was the most prominent landmark in the old city. It had the sarai, it had shops, coffee shops, hammam, it was an important public square.' She then went on to pull out the second map of Delhi which was dated 1914 by which time the British had made the city its capital. Here the entire road was marked in bold as Chandni Chowk. 'After 1857, the chowk itself is demolished by the British. The sarai goes and the hammam goes, so the significance of the chowk is completely gone. Perhaps once that was gone, the importance of that place was lost but the name remained and one started applying it to whatever was left,' she explained.

'What about the fact that almost the entire area that was previously Shahjahanabad is now loosely referred to as Chandni Chowk?' I asked her. 'I would have thought that the best name for it would have been Shahjahanabad. I have a feeling that in a very subtle way, the Mughal legacy was kind of down played. You need to remember that we are talking about a time immediately after the Partition. The whole demographic characteristic of Shahjahanabad changed drastically. A lot of Muslims had left. People who had come in, most from West Punjab set up their commercial enterprises there. It also became more Hindu and Jain. In that kind of an atmosphere, one somehow did not want this to be Shahjahanabad. One wanted this to be Chandni Chowk. Shahjahanabad suggests the Mughal Emperor Shah Jahan, whereas Chandni Chowk represents the commercial market,' she said. 'But you need to remember that this is my analysis, and it may or may not be true. A historian is after all like a detective. We have some evidence and we join the dots to underline a possibility.'

Historical analysis is often a plausibility, but not necessarily a certainty. Perhaps it was the aftermath of the Partition or maybe it was sheer chance as to why

Chandni Chowk came to be named so. What remains certain though is that in the course of four centuries since the time Shah Jahan built his dream capital, the shimmering moonlight on his favourite daughter's ambitious project had taken over the legacy of his name completely and had also managed to overtake the multiple little stories that went into its making.

In popular consciousness, Chandni Chowk conjures up images of romantic narrow streets, exotic shops, old havelis and delightful Mughal cuisine. To me though, Chandni Chowk is a name that carries within it, generations of history, pivotal episodes that have shaped and re-shaped Delhi in significant ways. The multitude of lanes and corners that make up modern Delhi's Chandni Chowk have stories to tell, of Shah Jahan's closest friends who lived in these quarters, of his most powerful administrative staff whose wealth and repute are still remembered in the names of the little neighbourhoods within Chandni Chowk, of the British capture of the city, of modern India's birth in the midst of its Partition and of the tales that went into the making of contemporary Delhi. Chandni Chowk in that sense, is not representative of any one history, but of several histories that have come together to mould it into what stands of it today.

However, what does the name mean to an insider,

someone who has lived for generations within the walled city of Shah Jahan and has observed the multiple changes it has undergone over time? My quest to understand the historicity behind the naming of Chandni Chowk took me to the house of Ashok Mathur who lives in Roshanpura at Nai Sadak, which is a street that runs close to the Chandni Chowk market. A tall, dark, broad shouldered man, in his 50s, Ashok was previously a journalist by profession. At present he busies himself with social work and by spreading awareness of the rich culture and history of Old Delhi.

On a bright winter afternoon, he sat down with me in his more than a hundred years old mansion to discuss how he has seen Old Delhi change over the years. Ashok's house is the quintessential Old Delhi haveli, that his family has dwelled in for the last six generations. He takes immense pride in its heritage and puts in effort to retain the original look and experience of the gorgeous pillars, arches and the large open courtyard.

Ashok's grandfather's uncle was brought in by the British from Mansaur in Madhya Pradesh and he worked in the notary. When asked what his ancestors would have called this place, he laughed and said, 'You know we still refer to this place as sheher (city). My uncles and cousins who have moved out, still call this place sheher. You see this was an entire civilization. There was nothing outside it except perhaps parts of old Mehrauli,' he explained further on sensing my confusion.

Reminiscing all the things he missed about the past

of Old Delhi, Ashok spoke out loud his concerns of the language and demographic changes this area has seen. 'There was a time when we could not imagine that Punjabi would ever be spoken on the streets of Old Delhi. It was either Hindavi or Urdu with a smattering of slangs like *oye* and *abe*,' he said. He went on to explain how the demographics of the area had changed over the years with most of his community members moving out due to excessive commercialization of this space.

The neighbourhood in which Ashok lives, Roshanpura, has an interesting history to it. Though it was predominantly occupied by Kayasthas, the area got its name from a rich Jain banker named Tansuk Rai Roshan whose house happened to be located there.

'But what about the fact that broadly any area inside Old Delhi is now referred to as Chandni Chowk?' I asked him, pondering over how a resident interacts with the history behind the naming of his neighbourhood. Ashok resentfully agreed with me, but added that 'Only ignorant people would call my neighbourhood as Chandni Chowk. If I am talking to a real Delhiwala, I would say we live in Roshanpura. To people who don't know this place, we have to tell them that we live in Chandni Chowk,' explained Ashok. 'Even a Google map on Uber calls this place Chandni Chowk, whereas Chandni Chowk is only that one street. We are not sitting in Chandni Chowk right now,' he said visibly disturbed with the phenomenon. 'If we now broadly start calling every place in Old Delhi as Chandni Chowk then so many names are lost. When a name is lost, its history is lost and when a history is lost then what is left?'

In November 2018, the name of Faizabad district was changed to Ayodhya.[25] Up until then, Ayodhya was a town in Faizabad district, the most popular one of course, because of its association with Lord Ram. A month earlier, the historic city of Allahabad too met with a similar fate when its name was changed to Prayagraj.[26] An ancient pilgrimage site for Hindus, Prayagraj, was always a part of Allahabad that had over centuries grown to accommodate the Mughal past within it.[27] As I end my conversation with Ashok, I am forced to wonder that hundred years down the line, if the history of India is written, how would the naming of Ayodhya and Prayagraj be recollected? Would the story of Lord Ram wipe away the multiple little stories that went into making Faizabad? Would the saffron mood of the country be accounted for while writing the origins of Prayagraj? The name of a place does carry within it a large amount of history, but what about the politics of it? When Shah Jahan dreamt of Shahjahanabad, could he ever have imagined that the shimmering moonlight would someday shadow over this entire city?

Connaught Place

An unremarkable British scion won over the heart of Delhi

LTD

Who was Prince Arthur, Duke of Connaught and Strathearn? Surely, a very important person in Delhi! Why else would his name occupy the heart of Delhi? In the more than 70 years following the independence of the country, efforts have been made to wipe out British names of numerous roads in Delhi. But the Duke of Connaught's presence in the hearts and minds of the people of Delhi has remained unshakeable.

Where can one find one of the oldest and best bakeries in the city, the finest of fabric brands, some of the most sought-after corporate spaces, old bookshops and of course a range of flea markets? The roundabout in the centre of modern Delhi, Connaught Place, has immortalized the last surviving son of the empress of British India, Queen Victoria for close to a century now.

At the onset of this chapter, I had carried out a social experiment to determine how many visitors and lovers of Connaught Place (more popular as CP) were aware of who or what Connaught was. As impressive as it got, the majority of my respondents were indeed aware of the fact that Connaught, as in the Duke of Connaught, was part of the British royal family. But that is about just as much that anyone knows about Prince Arthur. Some mistakenly assume that he is the brother of King George V, and many are clearly unaware of what exactly his association with Delhi or India is.

His name, or rather his title, however, has retained an unflinching popularity in Delhi. In the mid-1990s, there was an attempt by the Congress government in the centre to strike off the name of the royal scion, and replace it with that of Rajiv Gandhi—the descendant of yet another powerful family, but of course an 'Indian' one. Unfortunately, though, 'Rajiv Chowk', as the commercial complex was sought to be renamed, gained popularity only in terms of the nearest metro station. Connaught Place or CP stuck on in the popular consciousness of the people of Delhi, as one among the several residues of the British past which successive Indian governments struggle to shake off, largely unsuccessfully.

There is a term, 'colonial hangover', used popularly to describe the peculiar love-hate relationship that Indians share with their erstwhile rulers. A most perfect example of this ambiguous relationship is the unabashed promotion of English as the language of the privileged and educated, a mastery over which is understood to be of prime importance for any aspirant of social mobility. The popularity of the Duke of Connaught, devoid of any memory of who precisely he was, can very well be explained as a product of this very 'colonial hangover'.

It is the strange love for the British past which gives 'Connaught Place' a semblance of a higher and newer class. Perhaps this can explain why the owner of India Arts Palace, one of the oldest shops in the market had once mentioned the reason behind their preference for 'Connaught Place' over 'Rajiv Chowk'—'"Chowk" is not something you associate with a place as modern as this. For instance, it is okay for Chandni Chowk to be called so, but not for CP.'

But there is also the issue of the larger role played by the British in constructing Indian society as it exists today. Right from providing the country with its language of aspiration to giving it the first railways, postal services and also a model for governance, the contribution made by the English has had far-reaching consequences upon the way India functions today. For that matter, one can safely say that for the multiple religious, cultural and linguistic groups that constitute this unique country, the British rule and the fight against it, has probably served as the sole unifying factor. India, in that sense, is indeed a British construct.

Consequently, a large number of controversies arising out of socio-political and cultural differences in the country continue to be resolved by clutching on to a safer British past. Take for instance the anti-Hindi protests which had erupted in southern India in the 1950s and later in the 1960s when Hindi was proposed as the official language of the country. The protests were led by the Dravida Munnetra Kazhagam (DMK) in Tamil Nadu. The conflict was finally resolved when the then Prime Minister, Jawaharlal Nehru, enacted the Official Languages Act of 1963 which ensured the continued usage of English as the associate official language of the country, with Hindi being the official language and all other major languages of the country were given 'scheduled languages' status.

In the India of the 1990s when the country was just beginning to feel the rise of political parties ideologically opposed to the Indian National Congress, the proposal to rename CP as Rajiv Chowk was swiftly met with the criticism of being an act of sycophancy. Honouring Rajiv Gandhi was of course seen as a means of gratifying the most powerful political party in the country, but a continued commemoration of the son of Queen Victoria was just safer and politically untainted in independent India.

But coming back to the question with which I began this chapter, who indeed was the Duke of Connaught? Apart from being the son of Victoria and a chance visitor to the subcontinent right when CP was being made, there is in fact very less to his credit in terms of his association with Delhi. But then this also raises the question as to what precisely was the relationship that Indians and even the British shared with the royal family. The practice of naming places and institutes after members of the royal family, right after they visited, was almost steeped in tradition during the era of British rule.

On 17 January 1942, *The New York Times* carried an obituary for the Duke of Connaught who died at the age of 91. Spread over a quarter page of the newspaper, the

article noted the conditions in which the duke passed away, and glossed over the spectacular military career of the scion. Interestingly, it is only in the last paragraph (merely three sentences) of this grand commemorative piece that the mention of the duke's visit to India find a place.[1]

Of course, despite it being a short visit to the subcontinent, the duke had an important task to carry out. He opened, on behalf of the British sovereign, the new chamber of princes, the council of states and the reformed Indian legislative assembly in New Delhi.[2]

The obituary in *The New York Times* explained the choice of the duke for this 'prestigious' task as 'no member of the royal house possessed a greater or more detailed knowledge of India.' However, if official correspondence of the period is to be believed, then it would make clear that the Duke of Connaught was not the first choice for this royal visit which was being planned for about a year.

It was Edward VIII, Prince of Wales, the son of the then king of United Kingdom, George V, who was originally supposed to visit the subcontinent and carry out the inauguration of the war memorial, the chamber of princes as well as the council of states and the Legislative Assembly.[3] In fact, well into the second half of 1920, preparations were in full swing to welcome the prince, with details being put out about the kind of honours which can or cannot be presented to him.

It was only in August or September of 1920 that

the decision was taken to replace the son of the king-emperor, with his uncle, the Duke of Connaught. Incidentally, as opposed to what the duke's obit would have us believe, it was definitely not the 'detailed knowledge' of India that led to him being sent to New Delhi. Rather, it was simply a matter of chance that the Prince of Wales was facing health concerns which resulted in his visit being deferred.

Thereafter, the Duke of Connaught made his presence in the British new capital in February 1921, inaugurated the parliamentary houses announced in the 'Government of India Act, 1919', and as a token of honour, his name came to be enshrined forever in the new commercial complex being set up by the makers of New Delhi. Had things gone ahead as planned, who knows, Connaught Place might very well have been 'Wales Place' or 'Edward Circle'.

But this is not to say that the Duke of Connaught was without merit. The third son of Queen Victoria indeed has a very special place in the history of the British army and was fondly called the 'soldier prince'. The epithet was perhaps granted to him because he was known to have shown a particular affinity to a career in the military services right from his days of childhood.

The military contributions of the duke spread far and wide across the empire. Apart from India, he dedicatedly served in the Mediterranean, South Africa and of course in Canada.[4] In Canada, in fact, he had a rather distinguished role to play as the first member of the royal family to be given the title of 'governor-general'.

What appears to be his only biographical study mentions that 'he was destined to be the governor-general in that great realm in time to inaugurate in 1911, a new era of political development, prosperity and commercial expansion, and three years later to bear his part in the same great office during a period of intense loyalty and of self-sacrifice to a cause common to the whole empire.'[5]

Canada, in turn, has been more than grateful for the duke's significant presence in the country's history by etching his name upon a neighbourhood in the city of Calgary and a street well-known for its nightlife and cozy restaurants in Montreal.

While Canada indeed has much to commemorate the duke for, in India, the figure of the prince would almost pale in contrast to what so many other British officials have had to offer. One might safely say, that apart from laying his royal feet upon Indian soil, thrice in his 91 years of existence (the duke was serving in the army in Bengal between 1886 and 1890 as the commander-in-chief and in the 1903 Delhi Durbar he represented his brother, King Edward VII), there was very little he did to find himself an immortal place bang in the centre of the national capital.

I must also mention here about the nature of the relationship that the empire, particularly its manifestation in India, shared with the royal family. It is a well-known fact that the British crown's control over the Indian dominion intensified only after the liquidation of the power of the English East India Company in 1858. How this transfer of power might have changed the idea of sovereignty among the common people of India is hard to tell. The royalty lived a great distance away, making its grandeur felt only in the imaginations of Indians.

In circumstances like these, the royal visits had a special role to play. Historian Miles Taylor in his most recent book, *The English Maharani: Queen Victoria and India* makes an interesting observation as he writes, 'Royal visits made real the extent and purpose of the British Empire in India, emphasizing its military might and geographical girth, its durability in the shape of two generations of heirs to their throne and its modernity as its itineraries featured ceremonial openings of new railway lines, docks and other public works.'[6] In other words, the royal visits provided shape to the idea of the British crown, which until then was mostly restricted to the confines of fantasy.

It is worth noting how the temporary nature of the visits were given a semblance of permanency with names of institutes, roads and neighbourhoods commemorating the short presence of royalty in India. Queen Victoria, of course, needed to offer no such tour to have her name inscribed over innumerable parts of the subcontinent. It is fairly well known that the British monarch never travelled and it is equally remarkable that despite her near stationary presence in Britain, she happens to be one of the most commemorated people across the globe. From mini green patches, to giant-sized parks, schools, hospitals; from busy streets and markets, to entire cities and states across the world have been carrying her name with utmost diligence and respect through centuries.

Delhi too had a road named after the queen close to where the Parliament exists. However, it was renamed after Independence to commemorate the first president of the country, Rajendra Prasad.

In case of the empress's progeny, it became a practice to retain their names in some or the other form soon after they visited. Take for instance, the visit of Prince Albert Victor, grandson of Queen Victoria which took place in the winter of 1889–90, believed to be the most extensive of royal visits as he toured from Bombay to Travancore in the south, to Burma in the east and to Rawalpindi in the north-west.[7]

While at Mysore, in November 1889, Prince Albert laid the foundation stone of the glass house at Lal Bagh where horticultural shows were to be held. Soon after, as a mark of commemoration, the road from present day KC Circle to the Hardinge Circle came to be named as 'Albert Victor Road'. From Mysore, the prince travelled to Bangalore, and his name sits upon the 'Silicon Valley of India' as well, upon a road at Chamrajpet.

Prince Alfred, the second son of the Empress, made the first royal visit to the country in 1869. Being the first ever of its kind royal visit, the event was marked with much anticipation. *The Times of India* carried a report making a grand announcement of his visit in the words, 'There is a feeling of affection and reverence, vague but strong, among the natives of India, especially the higher classes, for Victoria and her family. We have no doubt that people would come from afar to do honour to him, and that his progress through the country would be something of a triumphal one.'[8]

The Prince spent four months touring across the length and breadth of the country and in memory of the visit, his name was given to the Rajkot High School, which is known to be the first English school in the Saurashtra region, more popular as the school from which the father of the nation, Mahatma Gandhi passed out.

The Duke of Connaught, was not just a royal visitor, but also a royal resident. He was the only member of the royal family to serve in India during the queen's lifetime in the late 1880s. It is to be noted that the Duke's third visit to Delhi was preceded by the First World War and conversations about the lack of funds available to build a capital as grand as that promised by King George V in the imperial durbar of 1911 was thick in the air. In these circumstances, it was deemed necessary to set the impression of European magnificence as firmly as possible in the edifices of New Delhi.

On 9 February 1921, the Duke inaugurated the first session of the two assemblies in the temporary Secretariat built north of Shahjahanabad. A few days later, he laid the foundation stone of the legislative chambers. As historian R.G. Irving notes in his book, *Indian Summer: Lutyens, Baker and Imperial Delhi,* the duke in his speech at the foundation of the legislative chambers 'conjured visions of the Athenian acropolis, the Capitol at Rome, and proud Oriental cities of antiquity, asserting that every great civilization had created its enduring and tangible records.'[9] He further noted that the new capital would link the people of India to the greatness of the empire spread out across the globe under the benevolent protection of the British crown.

The message was clear—New Delhi was a creation of the British crown, crafted with the sheer intent of bringing India at par with the European model of grandeur and greatness. While the substance of this message was drawn out most thoughtfully by the crown and its officials, it was the Duke of Connaught whose regal hands carried it to the people of India. His visit, in that sense, was indeed momentous and what better way to capture it forever than placing the prince's name upon one of the most important and popular features of New Delhi?

In the ensuing years though, Connaught Place, went on to capture the spirit of European regalia that the British had envisioned for it, with much ease. Both in the minds of those who dwell and work at the market and in the perception of those outside, the Duke's name has come to be intimately tied up with everything that is Western, modern, and of course, 'sophisticated' about Delhi.

In the late eighteenth century, when the English architect, John Wood designed the Royal Crescent at Bath, the idea was to capture a bit of the Roman Colosseum in England. Graeco-Roman architecture had by then earned a new popular appeal in western Europe. The English, inspired by the grandeur in its simplistic design, were quick to appropriate the best of Graeco-Roman construction practices and create an architectural style of their own, known as the Georgian architecture, named after the first four British monarchs of the House of Hanover—George I, II, III and IV. The Royal Crescent is believed to be one of the best products of the Georgian style.

Less than two centuries later, when another British architect Robert Tor Russell was tasked to build a commercial precinct at New Delhi, it was the Georgian Royal Crescent that he decided to slice out for the new British capital.[10] Connaught Place, modelled upon the row of residential buildings in Bath, was an attempt by the British to bring European architecture, culture and style, etiquette and everything else to India.

It is not as if the British were experimenting with European architectural forms for the first time in India. Even a cursory glance at the erstwhile European quarters in the presidency cities of Calcutta, Bombay and Madras would reveal the attempt on the part of the Englishmen to create a space for themselves resembling everything they were most familiar with back home.

In case of Delhi though, when the British monarchs were building a new capital, they were careful to include a large range of Indian stylistic motifs imposed with British beliefs, to create a city meant for the Indian populace being ruled over. Yet, in case of CP, the 'Indian' elements seem starkly missing. Though built by Indian contractors, and run largely by Indian businessmen, CP was European in every possible way.

In the imagination of the residents of old and new Delhi in the nineteenth century though, CP was not just European, it was also royal and distinctive, a shopping centre meant for the rich and mighty.

Sikander Changezi has grown up near Jama Masjid in Old Delhi with the knowledge of being the descendant of the founder of the Mongol Empire, Genghis Khan. Stepping into his residence at Pahari Imli, I felt I was almost transported back in time, to a household featuring in author Ahmed Ali's classic, *Twilight in Delhi.* The novel, written in 1940, was a vivid description of Delhi in 1911 when the Mughal era had waned and the British were raising a new Delhi.

Sikander's haveli, with a large open courtyard, and a leisurely balcony where a carpet was spread out along with colourful silken bolsters was undoubtedly reminiscent of a day and age which now remains nowhere else except in literary and cinematic descriptions of the history of Delhi. A group of women in colourful salwar kameez, resting on the bolsters and chatting away on a lazy autumn afternoon fitted in perfectly to complete the picture of *Twilight in Delhi*.

Indeed, Sikander himself was full of anecdotes and stories of the city in the era best described as its 'twilight'. His father, Naseem Mirza Changezi, who passed away in April 2018, was believed to have been the oldest living man in Delhi before his death. Sikander's story of Delhi is in fact largely a recollection of how his father engaged with it in his youth.

'My father had given shelter to Bhagat Singh when he was here in 1929 to throw a bomb at the Central Legislative Assembly,' said Sikander, his voice brimming with pride. He was equally delighted to inform me about how close his father was to the British residents in Delhi, including the family of the Anglo-Indian mercenary James Skinner, and that of the English civil servant William Fraser.

Sikander's father was born in 1912, at a time when the British were building a Delhi out of the ashes of Mughal glory. By the time Sikander was born in the late 1940s, independent India was both struggling to overcome a European hangover and at the same time looking forward to a bright and free future. Connaught Place or CP was barely a couple of decades old by the time of Sikander's birth.

The Old Delhi resident recalls how they would refer to the commercial precinct as 'lat ka market' (market of the lords). 'We would hardly go there. Everything was so expensive. Moreover, whatever we needed was available in Shahjahanabad,' he said. Sikander remembers his father telling him that despite the high prices, there were some things for which CP was the place to go to, for the best quality.

'My father would buy his shirts only from CP. Getting a shirt stitched in Old Delhi would cost us 6 annas and the same thing would cost 6 rupees in CP. But what shirts they were! Such beautiful fitting,' he recalled animatedly.

Other products like imported sportswear, gym equipment, coffee, pastries were also things that Sikander said he looked forward to during the occasional visit to the market. 'CP was meant for the British elite. They would travel to the market in cars. We in Old Delhi did not have any cars and would have to go there by tonga.'

Sikander's pride in his lineage is evident from the gusto with which he put on display the multiple creations of his family tree, the various Mughal era antiques in his possession, as well as all the tokens of honour given by the Indian government to his father for his contribution to the nationalist movement. 'My father fought valiantly for freedom because it bothered him that we were their slaves. But he also maintained that the British ruled over India efficiently and did a lot for the country's development.'

He kept silent for about a minute before asking, 'Why do we need to wipe away everything the British did over 200 years? Lord Willington Hospital has become Ram Manohar Lohia Hospital, Hardinge Library is now called Hardayal Library. If the government wanted to name a college after Nehru or someone else, they should just make a new college,' he says with a quiet thoughtfulness.

Connaught Place in fact continues to remain one of the most vibrant examples of British contribution to India's social and economic growth. Soon after the decision to build a new capital in Delhi was announced, representatives of the European commercial community in Calcutta demanded the creation of a shopping centre.[11] A commercial precinct in the middle of a city was an architectural practice found commonly in cities and towns of nineteenth-century England, and often, social life revolved around it.[12] Old Delhi's Kashmere Gate did function in a similar capacity previously, but CP was to be distinct in its European flavour and meant specifically for the British.

Yet, for all its European snobbery, much to the amusement of the residents of the 'walled city', there were hardly any people willing to open shops in CP once it was completed in 1933.[13] It was only during the Second World War that business picked up, as a large number of American and British soldiers made their way to Delhi and were quick to take a strong liking to all that CP had to provide.[14]

Once favoured by the white-skinned foreigners, the market was soon favoured by Indian businessmen who rightly saw in it a bright future. Some of them were Europeans and successful Indian businessmen who were running their shops in Old Delhi previously. Majority of the shops in CP though, were opened by far sighted businessmen from other parts of the country.

After its completion, the first shop to be opened was a departmental store by a Parsi businessman. However, the shop shut down soon after due to lack of sufficient business.[15] Wenger's, the bakery owned by a Swiss couple, followed. While it was already functioning in Kashmere Gate from 1924, its popularity among the British troops ensured that Wenger's had marked out a space for itself in A-block of CP right from the time the arcade was being built. Before Independence, the bakery had a largely British clientele who were in love with their chocolate, pineapple, vanilla and strawberry pastries along with the large varieties of bread the store had to offer. The bakery also had a ballroom on its first floor, making it a hugely popular wedding destination for the British and Anglo-Indian population of Delhi.

Presently, though the bakery is owned by the Indian businessmen Atul Tandon and his cousin Aman Tandon, the European legacy of the shop continues to reflect in the choice of its upmarket Delhi clientele who have an unshakeable attachment to their patties, pastries and cakes.

Wenger's is equally popular among international and national news publications. Enthusiastic reporters, eager to give a taste of the European past of Delhi to its readers, have often found themselves gloating upon the legacy of this bakery. I too have been guilty of pitching the story of Wenger's to my editors on numerous occasions, only to be curtly rejected, 'It has been written too many times and in too many publications.' Each of these numerous reports though, carry a uniform statement by the present owners who say that the ropes of the trade and its products have remained largely European, with some minute 'desi' additions being made over the years.

Yet another famous residue of the British era currently existing in CP is the United Coffee House. It was an Indian though who conceptualized it as a place where people from diverse backgrounds would meet in the evenings over coffee and snacks. Liquor baron, Lala Hans Raj Kalra, had first set up ventures in Sialkot and Lahore. When he moved to Delhi, he established the Esplanade restaurant at Chandni Chowk in 1938–39, specifically for the American soldiers stationed at the Red Fort barracks. However, once the war ended, his clientele left the city and the restaurant died out.

An astute businessman, Kalra was quick to gauge the potential of a similar white-skinned foreigner customer base in the newly set up shopping arcade.

Consequently, he opened the United Coffee House in CP in 1942.[16]

With its laidback fine dining atmosphere, large chandeliers and a turbaned watchman at the entrance saluting every diner moving in and out of the space, the restaurant continues to offer a slice of colonial era life in Delhi. In fact, the menu in United Coffee House has a substantial space dedicated to European delights hard to locate anywhere else in the city. Their cheese balls, chicken ala kiev, chicken maryland, mutton cutlets were and continue to remain hugely popular. Added to the list were Old Delhi charms, which the British had grown to take a liking to over time like chana bhatura, samosas, tikkas etc. Over the years, the menu has been expanded vastly to include dishes and flavours from across the country, thereby doing justice to its name. However, its old European feel has continued to remain the hallmark of the United Coffee House.

Post Independence, Wenger's and the United Coffee House are among the few odd old-time establishments remaining in CP. The dry-cleaning firm Novex, established in 1937 by two Mathura-based businessmen, the India Arts Palace opened in 1935 by the Backliwals who had their establishments in Chandni Chowk previously, the toy shop Ram Chandra and Sons set up by Raj Sunder who came to Delhi from Kasauli in 1935 are some of the extant remnants of a time when CP was just an infant with a promising future ahead.

In retrospect, one can perhaps suggest that the range of shops and the diversity of the owners' backgrounds was of significance to the history of the city. Connaught Place marked a shift in the commercial politics of a city that had long been in the shadow of a diminishing Mughal power. The new shopping complex had not only thrown open opportunities for enterprising individuals across the country, but had also brought back to the city its days of prosperity last seen under Emperor Shah Jahan. Previously, a similar commercial model was visualized in the city, that of Chandni Chowk designed by Jahanara Begum.

Despite the similarities in their socio-political framework, Connaught Place was no Chandni Chowk. The differences between the two is much the same as that between the structure and design of New Delhi and Shahjahanabad. If the latter is cluttered and organic, the former reeks of planned precision and administrative control. Equally interesting to observe is the difference in the social fabric and narratives offered by the occupants of both the spaces.

It was with much difficulty that I finally managed to arrange an interview with one of the old shop owners at CP. It is not as if the owners of these legacy stores of Delhi are shy of getting published, but rather it is the over reportage of the history of CP that acts as a deterrent. The extraordinary popularity of the place can perhaps be attributed to its location, bang in the middle of the city and close enough to the headquarters of almost every major newspaper and magazine, or maybe it is the exotic appeal attached to its past that has resulted in the history of the shops at CP being written and re-written just too often. The exhaustion with the interest in CP's past is almost palpable in the look and tone of almost every person associated with it. It is unsurprising then that most shop owners I reached out to responded to my requests with a swift and firm 'no, we have done this too many times in the past'.

I was therefore rather relieved when Satish Sundra, the owner of the toy shop Ram Chandra and Sons, agreed to speak with me. A fragile looking man in his 80s, Sundra, like most of his colleagues in the market, is evidently habituated to writers, researchers and journalists walking up to him for a glimpse into the world that CP was in its yesteryears. Sitting at his counter surrounded by toy cars, barbies, soft toys and every other childhood delight, Sundra was busy balancing his accounts when I walked in. He might very well be happy to share the managerial responsibility of his little shop with his son and daughter-in-law, but the final word on what Ram Chandra and Sons is and will be, continues to remain just his.

Of course, what Ram Chandra and Sons is to Sundra is evident from a brief interaction between him and a customer I happened to witness in the course of my interview. A young gentleman looking for a specific kind of toy laptop was visibly distressed at not being able to find it in Sundra's shop. 'Shops in Sadar Bazaar have it. How is it not available in your shop?' he asked with much annoyance. 'Please go buy from Sadar Bazaar itself,' came a prompt response from Sundra.

Once the gentleman had left the store, Sundra turned to his daughter-in-law and remarked, 'I do not like arguing with people who compare my shop to those in Sadar Bazaar.'

Sundra's pride in his shop is to do with its long and rich past, as well as with the illustrious clientele that he is accustomed to serving for the last many decades. 'I have served royalty here. Top politicians would come to this shop, so would all the rajas and maharajas and nawabs of the princely states. Connaught Place was built for the elite and rich,' Sundra said to me with a straight-faced resignation to a time gone by.

However, Sundra explained that most shopkeepers in CP were not rich, 'They built Connaught Place with sheer hard work and honesty.' Sundra's shop, Ram Chandra and Sons, opened at CP in 1935. His family started out their business from a shop at Ambala cantonment in 1890, from where it branched out to several cities including Kasauli, Delhi and later Chandigarh.

Sundra's narration of the story of his shop is a practised one. Clearly, he has recounted it on several occasions, the description of his family's days of penury in CP when his parents along with their three children would reside at the rear end of the shop. Despite the struggle, he maintained that 'living here was luxury'.

'There was a certain character to Connaught Place. I remember, every cinema theatre here would have a bar inside it. Couples would come to watch cinema and then get a drink in the bar afterwards before going for dinner. Years later, when I visited Paris, I realized that the culture was so similar there. Connaught Place reeked of a European aura, it was made by the British and for the British,' said Sundra in his usual practised narrative style.

When asked about the Duke of Connaught, Sundra quickly shook his head, 'Well, of course, he had nothing to do with India. But then the name is a symbol which opens up a broad vista of what was happening at that time and how this market was created. For us, the Duke of Connaught meant nothing, but the word is emblematic of the spirit of trust and hope that this place meant to us.'

*

21 May 1991 has been recorded in the pages of Indian history as a particularly significant moment. The scion of the Nehru-Gandhi family, and the Congress leader Rajiv Gandhi was brutally assassinated on this date. The savage political execution was carried out by a woman later identified as Thenmozhi Rajaratnam. She had been assigned to carry out the task by the chief of Liberation Tigers of Tamil Eelam (LTTE), Prabhakaran, in response to Gandhi's decision to send Indian peacekeeping forces to Sri Lanka at a time when animosities between the Sinhalese and the Sri Lankan Tamils had grown substantially.

Rajiv Gandhi's death, of course, was monumental in influencing the course that the Congress party would take in years to come, but the years preceding this incident had already paved the way for the social and political fabric of India to alter significantly. Historian Ramachandra Guha in his pathbreaking analysis of post-Independence India, *India After Gandhi*, has rightly noted that 'even by the standards of Indian history, the 1980s were an especially turbulent decade.'[17] As Guha further writes, 'The republic had always been faced with dissenting movements; but never so many, at the same time, in so many parts of India, and expressed with such intensity.'

While regional movements in Assam, Mizoram, Punjab, West Bengal and Jammu and Kashmir were simmering with its greatest intensity, the debate over the Shah Bano case and the Uniform Civil Code, as well as of course the long rallying call for a Ram temple to be built at Ayodhya, had gathered powerful momentum in ensuring disenchantment with the Congress party like never before. Further, the Bofors scandal that broke out in April 1987 and Gandhi's decision in September 1988 to introduce a bill aimed at controlling the freedom of the press, had only assisted in scarring the image of the prime minister further.

The impact was felt electorally soon, when in the elections of 1989, the Congress party won only 197 seats, down by more than 200 in their previous term. Thereafter, when Gandhi was assassinated in 1991, he had already lost the popularity he was once showered upon by the people of India who saw in his last name the credibility to be able to carry on the legacy left behind by his mother and grandfather.

It was in this moment of disillusionment with the Congress, and in the aftermath of the assassination, that a suggestion came from within the ranks of the party to erase the name of the British prince from the central market-place in Delhi and commemorate instead the prince of the Nehru-Gandhi family. The suggestion did not come from a family member, but rather a party leader and member of parliament, Mani Shankar Aiyer.

Aiyer joined politics only in 1989, before which he was part of the Indian Foreign Service. Apart from being a member of parliament for the course of three terms, Aiyer is also reputed as a political columnist and has authored several books, a majority of which happen to be about Rajiv Gandhi.

A staunch believer of Nehruvian policies, Aiyer's fascination with the Congress party, and his closeness with the Nehru-Gandhi family had developed since his years of childhood. His friendship with Rajiv Gandhi is known to have first blossomed during his school days at Doon School in Dehradun, where the latter was his junior, and then continued well into his college days at Cambridge. It is but natural that at the phase of his career when he joined politics, Aiyer worked very closely with Gandhi.

It was perhaps an ode to his friendship at the moment of Gandhi's death, that he suggested the renaming of Connaught Place as Rajiv Chowk, and subsequently asked for Connaught Circus to be named as Indira Chowk so that the two concentric circles would figuratively mean 'a mother embracing her son'.

While Aiyer's suggestion did pass through in official terms, it was soon met with massive criticism from both the opposition and the public, who called it out as an act of sycophancy. Heated arguments ensued on the nature of importance that the Nehru-Gandhi family held in the country, to the extent that during a parliamentary session, a BJP MP asked, '*Kya yeh desh Indira aur Rajiv ki jagir hai?* (Is this country the fiefdom of Indira and Rajiv?),' to which a Congress MP replied, 'Yes'.[18]

But though the name change did take place in official correspondence, it did not really gain popular acceptance. Apart from a handful of official buildings and of course the extremely busy metro station, hardly anyone ever favours Rajiv Gandhi over the British prince when it comes to the favourite market-place of the city. Even as recent as December 2018, the act of renaming had come under criticism when a group of 1985 Sikh riot survivors defaced a Rajiv Chowk sign board, demanding the market to be renamed as Connaught Place or to be named after the revolutionary leader, Bhagat Singh.

The lack of support for the renaming of CP is quite intriguing considering the fact that there are about 50–60 areas and objects of significance across the country which have been named after the former prime minister. The list includes hospitals, awards, airports, universities, schemes and others. The list is equally alarming when it comes to spaces named after Indira Gandhi. Why then would these two circles in the heart of Delhi reject their names in favour of a prince the people of the city had hardly anything to do with?

No one would be better suited to solve this puzzle than the man behind the name change proposal. Having lost out on his parliamentary seat in the 2014 general elections, Aiyer has been rather invisible on the political spectrum. His name has occasionally made news, but mostly as part of heated controversies, the most recent one being in 2017, when he called Narendra Modi a '*neech aadmi*' while campaigning during the Gujarat assembly elections.[19] His remark did not just draw severe ire from the ruling party, but was equally criticized by the Congress as well, and resulted in him being sharply rebuked and finally suspended.[20] Less than a year later though, his suspension was revoked and he was warmly welcomed back to his party.[21]

Aiyer has been accustomed to controversies throughout his political career. On the one hand have been his attacks on the opposition, often to the embarrassment of his party, on the other hand, he has also drawn criticism from the public for questionable statements like that of mocking students from Hansraj College and Kirori Mal while giving a lecture at his alma mater, St. Stephen's college in 2011.[22]

Looking at his record of provoking the ire of the public with misplaced statements, I was quite apprehensive about approaching him for an interview on a subject that had caused quite a stir back when it was first proposed. However, I must mention here, that my interaction with him right from the moment I made the first call on his personal phone number, to the 40 minutes I spent chatting with him in his office at Jangpura, has been nothing but warm and insightful.

Aiyer's narration of the days when he proposed the name change, and the aftermath of it, is deeply reflexive and extremely honest. Given the lucidity of his language, I assumed the best way to gain an insight into the matter would be to take his words just as they were spoken, so here is a transcript of my interview with him.

AR: Why did you propose the name change in the first place and what happened afterwards?

Very few people seem to know why Connaught Place and Connaught Circus got so named. In Dehradun, where I was brought up, they in their attempt to imitate a big city had their own Connaught Place. But they called it 'Kanat' place. It is clear to me that, 'kanat' being a tent or a pandal, these people who were invited to set up pandals in functions were the ones who gave this word some meaning.

As a child I used to be rather amused at this small-town effort to imitate the metropolis. Then I came to the conclusion that maybe people accepted the name so easily because they associated it with 'kanat' or the tent-making business.

I don't know whether I am right or not but, in any case, it seemed to me to be extraordinary that we should, so many years after Independence, continue to name one of the most important marketplaces, after perhaps the least distinguished Englishman to visit India. The Duke of Connaught had practically no credit to himself, other than being the younger brother of the king.

The foundation stones for the new city of New Delhi which was to be the British equivalent of Shahjahanabad, Tughlaqabad, had to be laid, and the Duke of Connaught was deputed to come across to India for the purpose. Apart from this visit, he was an utterly undistinguished man who never again appears in history. The British then decided to call the marketplace that they were building in New Delhi as sort of the equivalent of Oxford Street, as Connaught Place and Connaught Circus.

The man came here and then went to Praetoria and inaugurated the parliament building that is there and in effect therefore, is responsible, for apartheid in Africa which affected adversely not only the Africans, but also the Indian community living there.

My point was, why should we be retaining the name 'Connaught' when several other Englishmen, who have made notable contributions to India have had their names removed?

For instance, we used to have a road named 'Queensway' which was changed to 'Janpath'. There was 'Kingsway' which was changed to 'Rajpath'. King Edward's Road became Maulana Azad Road, Victoria Road became Dr Rajendra Prasad Road, Hardinge Avenue was changed to Tilak Marg, King George's Avenue became Rajaji Marg, Curzon Road is now called Kasturba Gandhi Marg.

All over Lutyens' Delhi we have removed the names of the British and replaced them with names of Indian heroes.

I must add here, that I was six years old when Jawaharlal Nehru became the prime minister of the country, and I was 23 when he died in 1964, so I was brought up in the Nehruvian ethos, and regarded him as an extraordinary person. I continue to be a great fan and supporter of Nehruvian secularism, Nehruvian democracy and foreign policy. I was delighted when I found on the map of Delhi that Central Park which is in the middle of Connaught Place, was given the name 'Nehru Park'. It would appear that subsequently, the park outside Ashoka hotel was given the name Nehru Park, but I have seen maps of Delhi from an earlier date where it is clearly written that Central Park is now Nehru Park, in the memory of him after he passed away.

Now when Rajiv Gandhi passed away, it occurred to me that if the official name of Central Park is Nehru Park, then why not replace this utterly obscure Englishman's name. Why not rename Connaught Circus as Indira Chowk, and perhaps in a moment of excessive emotions, suggested that Connaught Place be named after Rajiv, so that eternally the mother's arms would be embracing the child, both of whom were assassinated. And with the grandfather in the centre, the entire family would be commemorated.

It is a family which back in 1990 did not have the least parallel to their importance in the nation-building of modern India. It was really between Nehru, Indira and Rajiv, who gave us the idea of modern India, which today is under serious challenge.

I had put the proposition at a rather sentimental moment. I had worked with Rajiv very closely. I made the proposal to the prime minister, Mr Narasimha Rao, who passed it on to SB Chavan and Chavan told me that I should also get Tajdar Babbar on board because she was the chairman of the New Delhi Municipal Corporation (NDMC). I approached Tajdar and the proposal went through the NDMC and then the Indian government.

But then there was a huge outcry, primarily from the shopkeepers, who had acquired the brand name of Connaught Place, and therefore did not want to lose that brand, but had no idea who Connaught was.

But I must confess that I failed in my attempt, because neither does anyone call Connaught Place Rajiv Chowk, nor is Connaught Circus called Indira Chowk. But I stuck to my guns. I got another opportunity when the Metro came up and I approached Sheila Dikshit to name the station there as Rajiv Chowk. She was as good as her word and named it so. Now with that station, which happens to be the most used metro station, being named Rajiv Chowk, I achieved my objective.

AR: Would you say that the outcry was because it was a Gandhi family member being commemorated?

It was all that. Don't forget, it was the mid-1990s and by that time Rajiv had been rejected by the people largely because of all the allegations which were made against him, none of which have been proven to be true. In the immediate aftermath of not only his defeat, but also the comeback, and the great push that the BJP had obtained under the aegis of V.P. Singh and Chandra Shekhar, the Congress had returned but Rajiv had not returned. So those on the anti-Congress front, of whom there were many, and those who belonged to the middle class of India which had grown very disenchanted by Rajiv, as well as the business circles involved in Connaught Place—they gathered together in protest against the memorialization of the Gandhi family.

AR: Why would you say that Rajiv Chowk did not take off among the people of Delhi?

The time was wrong. We were in decline. There was build up of a lot of the sentiments which has now exploded and the Congress party, then under Narasimha Rao, was not particularly interested in celebrating these two people at a time when there was considerable tension between Sonia Gandhi and them.

There was no enthusiasm inside the party. It was not a party initiative, but was seen more as an initiative by me.

Aiyer's statements substantiates one point very clearly—the contention over the name change of Connaught Place is symbolic of the political sentiments in India in the 1990s, and the beginnings of an era which is perhaps at its climax in current times.

Earlier this year when the BJP stalwart and former president of the Delhi and District Cricket Association (DDCA), Arun Jaitley, passed away, the DDCA decided to commemorate him by engraving his name upon what was then known as Feroz Shah Kotla stadium after the Turkish Muslim ruler of the fourteenth century. The former name of the stadium was established on account of its closeness to the palace built by the Tughlaq ruler in the fourteenth century which went by the name Feroz Shah Kotla.

The renaming of the stadium was yet again met with a debate. While some applauded the decision to honour the former finance minister, there were others who mourned the loss of a slice of medieval history, embedded as it was, in the name of the ruler known to have carried out some of the most spectacular architectural work in the city.

But haven't those in power always determined the heroes of history? Yet public memory is a different matter. The name that is closest to one's heart might well be historically inaccurate, or not even in line with the politics of the time, but still as we all know, 'the heart wants what it wants'. Only time will tell if Arun Jaitley will win over Feroz Shah Tughlaq in the consciousness of the people of this city, what we do know is that time could never wipe out the name of the Duke of Connaught from the heart of Delhi.

Chittaranjan Park

The favourite hero of the Delhi Bengali

Paritosh Bandopadhyay has vivid memories of the days when his 'Bangali colony' was being built. Since the 1950s he had been hearing rumours of such a space being carved out for Bengalis. He was a fresh migrant to the city at that time, having cleared the civil service examination. The thought of building his own home, in a neighbourhood marked out specifically for his own kind, had appeared irresistible to him. He immediately applied for allotment, was assigned a plot, and there he built his home in this city of hope.

'At that time there was only forest and thorny bushes here. The government had just started constructing the roads and laying out sewer lines. But the place had my heart. I was so proud of it. This was going to be our own neighbourhood. Our Bangali colony,' he recalled with a broad grin.

CR Park was simply called 'Bangali colony' at that time. Colloquially, it is still called the same. No name, just a piece of land meant for Bengalis. Any new Bengali migrant in Delhi knows that CR Park is the place where one can find a home away from home. It is the place where one can find noisy fish markets, sweet shops, frenzied Durga Puja celebrations and of course, neighbours and shopkeepers who will only communicate with you in the Bengali language.

It would be no exaggeration on my part to observe that the air around CR Park reeks of Bengali sentiment in every which way. Walk into any of the four main markets in the neighbourhood and you would be welcomed with old Bengali songs blaring inside restaurants and tea shops. Sights of the young and old huddled together over cups of tea, a carrom board and endless discussion on politics are hardly uncommon. Shops are lined up with the choicest of Bengali food items and ingredients that are hard to spot anywhere else in the city like *narkeler nadu* (a sweet dish made of grated coconut), *moa* (a sweetmeat delicacy made of puffed rice), *bori* (dried lentil dumplings) and many others. Stride around the residential blocks and you will be greeted with the sweet aroma of brinjal or fish being fried in fresh mustard oil.

And then there are the people. A tight knit Bengali community living in a land far away from Bengal and amidst many other communities, had meant that the CR Park Bengali tries a bit harder to preserve its culture. There was a time, I am told, when preparation for Durga Puja in the neighbourhood would begin six months in advance and with much gusto. The terrace of every house would be brimming with excitement as groups assembled prepared Bengali theatre, music or dance performances for the Durga Puja. The cultural commitment of the CR Park Bengali is perhaps the reason why residents from across the city throng into the neighbourhood to witness what it means to celebrate the annual worship of Goddess Durga the Bengali way. The community bonding of the neighbourhood is equally evident in the way residents address each other as '*dada*' (elder brother), '*didi*' (elder sister), '*mashi*' (maternal aunt), '*pishi*' (paternal aunt), giving the area a unique sense of being a single family.

Paritosh was one of the first residents of CR Park. I had met him at his home in B block, the same one that he had built when the colony was first established. With its large windows, two-winged doors, modest furnishings and shelves lined up with books, Paritosh's house had an uncanny resemblance to any north Kolkata home. Perhaps every Bengali carries a bit of Bengal with him wherever he or she goes.

He was working on his dining table at that time, with papers, books, magazines, newspapers, pens and pencils scattered all around. Paritosh had worked and retired as a journalist from the Press Trust of India. When I met him, he was in the process of penning down his rather exciting life in a series of travelogues consisting of his personal experiences in the 30 countries he had visited as part of his career. 'I am doing this so that I live on after I die. *Ami jaate furiye na jaayi* (so that I don't disappear into oblivion).'

Paritosh was one of the many people directly involved in the naming of CR Park. He told me all about how before the naming of the neighbourhood after the Bengali nationalist leader, Chittaranjan Das, it was labelled as 'East Pakistan Displaced Persons' Colony' (EPDP). The name was a very clear indication of the purpose behind building the neighbourhood and the people residing in it. Unlike what 'Bangali colony' would have you believe, this neighbourhood located on the

Outer Ring Road, was not meant for the Bengalis. It was actually meant for any person who had lost out on land and property in East Pakistan after the 1947 Partition of the country. Understandably, a majority of them happened to be Bengalis, giving this piece of southern Delhi a distinct eastern flavour.

Eventually though, the residents of EPDP colony wished to rename their neighbourhood from this rather unexciting and straightforward name to something more fitting of their history and identity. As Paritosh and many of my other interviewees narrated to me, the process was not an easy one. Several rounds of discussions and debates were held before zeroing down on Chittaranjan Das.

Leaders of the nationalist movement in India are the easiest to spot among the nameplates of a large number of streets and neighbourhoods in Delhi. Kamla Nagar (named after Kamala Nehru), Lajpat Nagar (named after Lala Lajpat Rai), Sarojini Nagar (named after Sarojini Naidu), Aruna Asaf Ali Marg (named after the famous political activist), Patel Nagar (named after Sardar Vallabhbhai Patel) are just a few among the hundreds of areas that carry names of freedom fighters.

Some among these were products of renaming sprees that independent India's new government engaged in, to wipe out the memory of a British Raj and replace it with the names of the heroes who helped achieve a free India. Kasturba Gandhi Marg for instance, was a name that replaced Curzon Road, named after the

British Viceroy. Then there were the new settlements that had to be created in order to make space for the Partition refugees coming in from Pakistan. These were ancient and medieval villages on the outskirts of the city, which were cleared out and their names replaced with a series of 'nagars' named after freedom fighters.[1] As noted by the celebrated Delhi history enthusiast, Sohail Hashmi, if the people had the agency to name their neighbourhoods, they would probably have preferred naming them after the places they left behind. But as the government developed these places, it named these new colonies after the historical icons they wanted to celebrate.[2]

Chittaranjan Park, better known by its abbreviation as CR Park, is part of the latter group. But among the refugee colonies of Delhi, CR Park was also unique since it was the only one that catered to the aftermath of the Partition as it unfolded in the eastern part of the country. In their choice of a name for their colony, residents of CR Park had to find a nationalist icon, that too one that best captured the essence of the freedom movement as it transpired in the place to which they traced their identities—Bengal. There was a large basket of names of immense repute to select from. Why did this group of displaced Bengalis settle upon Chittaranjan Das? What were the internal discussions taking place in order to decide upon the name which best encapsulated their historical identity? Was it truly their choice or one that the government chose for them?

Before I answer these questions though, let us take a step back and first look at how our 'Bangali colony' got its first name—EPDP. The name EPDP captured in a nutshell the unique history of this colony.

✻

Paritosh is a compulsive speaker. He loves speaking, at length and with lucid descriptions. At 87, he lives all by himself, his son, daughter-in-law and grandson occupying the floor above him. A bald figure, with a pair of square-rimmed spectacles atop his nose and a stick in his hand to help him walk, Paritosh is the quintessential image of a Bengali dadu (grandfather). And just like the stereotype of every grandfather-like figure, he is full of stories—of his childhood days in Faridpur (now part of Bangladesh), of the time when the ghastly Partition uprooted him and his family, bringing them to Calcutta, of his journey to Delhi to eke out a stable and successful future and of course, of the time he saw his beloved CR Park being built.

His journey from Faridpur to New Delhi is the classic CR Park Bengali story of Partition related displacement. He was born in Dhaka, a good 15 years before Independence. But he spent most of his childhood and adolescence years in Faridpur where his father worked as a school teacher.

Paritosh was in high school when political discussions around the Partition suddenly gained momentum.

There were no riots in Faridpur but he would often hear of riots and bloodshed in neighbouring towns and districts. 'The slogan, "*lad ke lenge Pakistan*" (we will fight for Pakistan) was a common one to be heard all around at that time,' he narrated. Despite there being no violence where he stayed, the prospect of a partition had instilled fear into his family. Well-wishers advised them to leave East Bengal in order to avoid any humiliation or harm.

'My father's Muslim students no longer respected him. They did not want him to teach there anymore and they wished to take control of the school's administration,' he recalled. A particular incident that shook him was that of one of the students calling the *azaan* in front of their house. 'This was an unusual spot for such an act of religiosity. We felt teased and humiliated,' he narrated before taking a moment of silence. 'They simply wanted to assert that this was their Pakistan now.'

A few days later, there were rumours about his father being issued an arrest warrant. Apparently, he had spoken out against Jinnah's two-nation theory at a public gathering which was being seen as an attack on Pakistan. Well-wishers of their family soon advised them to leave East Bengal in order to avoid any further humiliation. Paritosh's father first left with his two sisters for Calcutta, while he stayed back to complete his matriculation exams, after which he too left. He was 16 at that time.

As he spoke about his family's exodus, Paritosh became very emotional.

'My father had spent 32 years working at that school. He was a dedicated teacher and everyone in our village respected and loved him. Many of his students had grown up to be successful people.'

'Once he got onto the steamer, he had an emotional breakdown. He was leaving behind the village where he had spent the prime of his life and could not hold back his tears. He finally had just one line to say—*"Gandhiji tumi haira gele* (Gandhiji, you have lost").'

It was in Calcutta that Paritosh went on to complete his graduation and then appeared for the civil service examinations. He moved to Delhi in 1955 after clearing the examinations and acquiring a job at the Central Secretariat. CR Park or EPDP colony was still a distant dream at that time.

It is impossible to live and engage with Delhi without being aware of the resounding echoes of Partition that can be heard in almost every nook and corner of the city. A large part of this narrative though, is preoccupied with how the division of the country took place on the west. CR Park, in that sense, stands out in telling the story of the Partition of Bengal and the making of East Pakistan.

Unlike the west, where the Partition caused a sudden, violent upheaval of its population, in the east, the process was a lot more gradual with much less government intervention.[3] An estimated 5 million are known to have migrated to India from East Pakistan over a period of 18 years between 1946 and 1964.[4] The number almost pales in contrast to the approximately 7.5 million that crossed borders from West Pakistan to north India within a matter of three years.[5]

There was also a difference in the reception meted out to the two groups of refugees. Refugees from West Pakistan were the biggest beneficiaries of government aid and attention.[6] The city Chandigarh was built specifically for the purpose of settling refugees. In Delhi, as we saw earlier in this chapter, many settlements were drawn out especially for the purpose.

Mehr Chand Khanna was appointed minister of rehabilitation. His name is what gives Khanna Market and the adjacent Meherchand market their names, both markets carrying shops allocated to Partition refugees.[7] Khanna overlooked the process by which large swathes of agricultural fields around the old city were acquired and then cleared to make way for living quarters.

In the east, that was not the case. The lack of rehabilitation aid for the refugees is attributed to the fact that the power centre of a newly created India was in the north.[8] The government in West Bengal depended on the centre for directing resources for the rehabilitation of the refugees. 'The centre provided these resources grudgingly and too late, since it was preoccupied with the problem of resettling seven million refugees fleeing the massacres in the Punjab,' records historian Joya Chatterjee.[9] She further notes that Nehru himself was convinced that the situation in Bengal was not as grave. Consequently, no such settlement program was carried out in the east. Neither were cities built specifically for the purpose, nor neighbourhoods cut out in Calcutta as was done in Delhi.

Even academic scholarship on the refugee problem in the east has been quite limited. When the east did become the focal point of Partition narratives, it was a particular kind of refugee, namely the 'Bengali *bhadralok*' who became the object of interest. They were the educated upper-middle class, whose experience of the Partition was almost exclusively centred around the fear of violence, the loss of land, property and respect and nostalgic memories of the lost homeland.[10]

This was the class that was the first to leave East Pakistan either in the wake of the Partition or even before.[11] They are the key to understanding the way EPDP colony came into existence. A majority of them had moved to Delhi in search of jobs or, like Paritosh, were part of the government service and were posted in the city. For that matter, ever since the 1861 ICS Act was passed, which opened the doors of government jobs to Indians, the competitive examination ensured the recruitment of a majority of Bengali Hindus.[12]

Then there are those who are second or third generation Bengalis in Delhi, with no memory of having lived in East Pakistan. Their only claim to a piece of land in the 'Bangali colony' is that they had ancestral property in East Pakistan which they can no longer own on account of the Partition.

Consequently, when in the 1950s, the centre was busy rehabilitating the thousands of refugees from West Pakistan, few Bengali government employees in Delhi came to the conclusion that it was necessary for some form of compensation to be given to those who had lost out on their property in East Pakistan. The 'Association of Central Government Employees Dislodged from East Pakistan' was established in 1954 with this purpose. When they first approached the government for the allotment of some land or home to those employees who had been dislodged from East Pakistan, their demand was turned down with the argument that the number of such persons was too less and also that they did not have refugee certificates.

The association then realized the need for increasing membership and also that of involving higher officials in their pursuit. C.K. Mukherjee, one of the key representatives of the association, reached out to Ila Pal Chowdhury who was then a member of the Parliament. He convinced her to carry their concerns to Khanna. His argument was that these government employees who traced their ancestry to East Pakistan could no longer go there to claim their properties after retirement. In this context, the association also realized that using the phrase 'displaced persons from East Pakistan' rather than 'dislodged' or 'refugee' would better serve their purpose.[13]

International definition of 'refugee' is identified as one who 'owing to well-founded fear of being persecuted for reasons of race, religion, nationality, membership of a particular social group or political opinion, is outside the country of his nationality and is unable, or owing to such fear, is unwilling to avail himself of the protection of that country; or who, not having a nationality and being outside the country of his former habitual residence as a result of such events, is unable or, owing to such fear, is unwilling to return to it.'[14] The Bengali residents of Delhi demanding land allotment clearly did not fall in this category as they were in the city as government employees.

By now though, those displaced persons from East Pakistan who were entrepreneurs or were working in private companies were unhappy about being left out of this facility of land allotment. They too demanded to be made part of the association. Thereafter, it was decided that any person 'gainfully employed residing in the Union Territory of Delhi and displaced from East Pakistan' was eligible for membership of the association. Consequently, the name of the association was changed to 'East Pakistan Displaced Persons' Association' or the EPDP.[15]

Finally, as announced by the minister of rehabilitation, 218 acres of land in Kalkaji, adjoining Chirag Delhi, would be allotted for displaced persons from East Pakistan. This area was then named as 'East

Pakistan Displaced Persons Colony', or EPDP colony.

Paritosh was living in the government quarters at Vinay Nagar at the time, which is today better known as Sarojini Nagar. The naming of Vinay Nagar also has a fascinating story to it. Vinay, meaning politeness, was one of the principles propounded by the ancient Indian political philosopher Chanakya. In 1951, when the Ministry of Foreign Affairs was pondering over what to name the large expanse of land in Central Delhi which would be home to ambassadors from 44 countries and their embassies, Maharajakrishna Rasgotra who was then the assistant chief protocol at the ministry suggested the name, 'Chanakyapuri', after the ancient Indian philosopher. His reasoning was that the area must be named after the best-known authority on Indian diplomacy and foreign policy. Consequently, the roads that stem out of Chanakyapuri, cut out mainly for government housing, were named after the philosopher's principles—Shanti Path, Nyaya Marg, Vinay Nagar, Satya Marg and Niti Marg.[16]

EPDP colony would be Paritosh's seventeenth accommodation in Delhi. Apart from Vinay Nagar, he had lived in Gole Market where a large number of Bengalis lived after they came to Delhi, Lakshmi Nagar and Lodhi Road. 'When I heard about a "Bangali colony" being built, I immediately knew what a great opportunity this was for me,' he said with a wide smile. 'After putting in my application, I would frequently visit this place out of curiosity. I had no idea where my house had been allotted. But that was a beautiful feeling in knowing that this would be my place and for my people.' He finally shifted into his home in EPDP colony in 1971.

*

Bengali presence in Delhi today is considered almost synonymous with CR Park. Lesser known is the long history of Bengali-speaking residents of the city that goes back to the late nineteenth century. Delhi at that time, was primarily Shahjahanabad, which explains why the early Bengali settlers' imprint can be found in Old Delhi.

The first Bengali resident of Delhi as per records was Umacharan Basu from Chandannagar in West Bengal, who came here in 1837. Umacharan had enlisted himself in the Mughal army and was perhaps appointed in Delhi.[17] Three years later, the first Kali Bari came up at the spot where the Nigambodh Ghat exists today. Temples dedicated to Goddess Kali are almost an essential requirement of Bengali religious sentiments. Consequently, wherever the Bengali diaspora settled, the establishment of a Kali Bari became a subsequent development. The first Kali Bari of Delhi though was destroyed during the mutiny of 1857. The idol was later salvaged and placed at a temple in Roshanpura. It was only in 1917, that land for a new temple was bought at Tis Hazari where the Kali Bari was shifted and still exists today.[18]

Half a century after Umacharan, we come across the famous doctor Hemchandra Sen, whose name is given to H.C. Sen Marg which shoots out of the Chandni Chowk market. Sen is believed to have come to Delhi to attend a fair and remained here thereafter. He started his pharmacy in the fountain area of Chandni Chowk, which is marked as a symbol of the first commercial enterprise by Bengalis in Delhi.[19]

Another significant enterprise was started in 1883 by Aushutosh Ray of Jaipur. Ray started the Indian Medical Hall Press, which produced publications in Urdu, Persian and Arabic, which were widely used languages in Delhi. The business flourished for about a hundred years in the fountain area before shifting out to the newly developed southern part of the city. Ray's family lived in the area behind the Jama Masjid. This was also the place where Swaminath Banerjee, who began the Bengal Paper Mills, lived.

Then there were the ambitious businessmen who popularized Bengali sweets in Delhi. Panchanan Banerjee came to Delhi in 1913 in the hope of making a fortune. He is credited with establishing the first Bengali sweet shop in Delhi, also in the Chandni Chowk market, called the 'Kamalay Mishtanna Bhandar', which later got another branch in Gole Market. Another sweet shop, the Annapurna Bhandar, established by Mohini Mohan Mukherjee also came up in the fountain area of Chandni Chowk.

The shift of the capital from Calcutta to Delhi in

1911 ushered in a new phase in the history of Bengalis in Delhi. A large number of Bengali government employees shifted to the city. Parts of what is the North Campus of Delhi University today served as the viceroy's house soon after the shift of the capital. In Timarpur, nearby, government residence was made available to the employees who moved from Calcutta to the new capital.[20]

By the 1920s and '30s, a thriving Bengali community came to exist in areas like Kashmere Gate, Daryaganj, Timarpur, Karol Bagh, Chandni Chowk, Sadar Bazaar, Nai Sadak, etc.

Ruma Ghosh, who is currently a resident of CR Park, is one of those whose family had migrated to Delhi from Bengal in the early decades of the twentieth century. Her father, Shantiranjan Dutta Ray, had moved to the city from Comilla in East Bengal in 1936 looking for a job.

Ruma's father had settled in Kashmere Gate, which was the heart of Old Delhi at that time and a location where a large number of Bengalis were living. The neighbourhood got its name from the ornate gateway built by Emperor Shah Jahan to the north of the walled city and named it so because it faced the road that led to Kashmir. In the memories of Delhi's Bengali community though, the significance of Kashmere Gate lies in housing the oldest Bengali club in the city which was established in 1925, and hosting the first ever Durga Puja as well.

Ruma was born here in 1953. As she told me over

and again on several occasions, 'to me, the culture of Delhi Bengalis would always be the one that I grew up with in Kashmere Gate.' Tall, slender and astonishingly beautiful, Ruma is a veteran theatre artist. She also worked with All India Radio throughout her professional life. She told me about how her interest in theatre and culture grew out of the Bengali club, which would be the point of congregation for all Bengalis in Delhi.

From her childhood days itself, she had been hearing conversations around a colony being developed in the southern part of the city. 'My father was not at all keen to move to CR Park. He would be terrified thinking about moving so far away from the city into this forested area,' she said, laughing. Ruma recalled those days, 'During that time the workplace for most ordinary Bengalis was in Old Delhi,' she said. It was only in the early 1990s that she managed to convince her father to sign up for a plot in CR Park. 'But this is only the story of my father. Most Bengalis in CR Park were very happy to acquire a plot here.'

Ruma, however, had shifted to CR Park much before her father did, in the 1970s, after she got married. This was the time when the colony had just begun to sprout. 'Culturally, I felt uprooted to be honest,' she told me about her early days in CR Park. 'Perhaps because in Kashmere Gate we were a community living alongside several other communities, and because Bengalis in Old Delhi were centred around the Bengali Club, we had become very close-knit,' she explained slowly and with long pauses in between. 'In CR Park, the community was no longer this close-knit. Here we were too many Bengalis spread out over a large area. In Old Delhi, even though people lived faraway from each other, all Bengalis would come together and find common ground in the Bengali Club,' she explained.

This club, famous for having hosted Rabindranath Tagore during his visit to Delhi, was where Bengalis of the city found their cultural identity through music, dance, theatre, sports and festivals ranging from the Bengali New Year, Rabindra Jayanti, Saraswati Puja and of course, the Durga Puja. Ruma remembered her disappointment in finding that every block in CR Park had a separate Durga Puja. 'I don't remember a time when all Bengalis of CR Park congregated in a single puja. That kind of interaction and close bonding was missing here,' she said.

Nonetheless, the establishment of EPDP colony was a fresh phase in the history of Delhi's Bengalis. Hitherto, though the community existed in large numbers in certain neighbourhoods of Old Delhi, there was no one area which was just defined by Bengalis. EPDP colony became that space—a slice of Delhi that was completely Bengali.

Consequently, it had to be given a name appropriate enough to capture both the Bengali identity of its residents and their history of losing land and property due to the Partition of the country. When the question of naming first arose, the residents began weighing out their options among the large number of celebrated Bengali personalities who were part of the freedom movement. Two names were the initial favourites—the Bengali literary giant and Nobel laureate Rabindranath Tagore, and nationalist revolutionary hero Netaji Subhas Chandra Bose. Both options, however, were dropped soon after. By the 1970s, Delhi already had Tagore Park named after the former, and Netaji Nagar had come up carrying the name of the latter.

Then there was another name that was incidentally more popular among those who had initially voted for the colony to be named after Tagore. This was '*Purbanchal*' which translated as 'mountain ranges of the east'. The name was to be a reminder of where the residents of EPDP colony came from.

Ranajit Raychaudhury, a resident of I block in CR Park told me that the residents had in fact accepted the official name of the neighbourhood as Purbanchal. Ranajit was born in the village, Chandpur in East Bengal, and had moved to Calcutta with his family after the Partition. Like Paritosh, he too moved to Delhi in the 1950s after clearing the civil services examination and was one of the first few applicants for a plot in EPDP colony. 'Most of the surrounding areas here were occupied by the Punjabis who came from the west. We wanted to assert the fact that we were different in that we belonged to the east,' he said to me.

But not everyone was happy with the name. There were some who pointed out the fact that Purbanchal referred to mountains. Neither did it describe accurately the place of origin of the neighbourhood's residents, nor did it signify in any way the new home they had built in Delhi.

There was also the problem of a political controversy hanging over the name. Purbanchal was the name proposed for a new state by the Bengali-speaking people of Barak Valley in southern Assam. This region had seen a large inflow of immigrants from East Pakistan in the wake of the Partition. The proposition was met with violent protests and created a disturbing rift between the Barak Valley and the rest of Assam, one that continues to exist till date. This conflict between the Bengali immigrants and the local population of Assam came to the forefront very recently when the Citizenship Amendment Act (CAA) was passed by the Indian government.

Back in the 1960s and '70s though, the separatist movement in southern Assam and the political tensions it had created in the North-east was still very fresh. Consequently, it was but natural for the residents of EPDP colony to avoid being associated with a name that was already a source of much conflict in a different part of the country, that too in a state bordering their original homeland.

The other choice for a name that emerged by now was that of Chittaranjan Das. Popularly called 'Deshbandhu' (friend of the nation), Das was a freedom fighter and lawyer who helped defend several nationalist revolutionaries during the struggle for Independence. Das was born and raised at a time when the Bengal renaissance (a cultural, social and intellectual movement in Bengal under British influence in the nineteenth century) was at its peak.

Das's introduction to politics happened after he moved to England having completed his graduation in 1890 to appear for the ICS examination. He spearheaded agitations against the humiliation meted out to the Indian community in England. It was during this time that Das's anti-colonial political ideology was shaped.

After returning to India as a barrister, Das got involved in the revolutionary movement taking shape here. He came in touch with the revolutionary leader Aurobindo Ghose who later became his spiritual guru and initiated him into the organization 'Anushilan Samiti' which mothered several other secret societies in Bengal, Maharashtra, Punjab and others.

In the relatively short span of his political career, Das was directly involved in the nationalist movement in multiple ways. Apart from revolutionary activities, he also provided support to the non-cooperation movement of 1919–1922, was a strong proponent of the Swadeshi movement, founded the Swaraj party in 1923, along with Motilal Nehru and H.S. Suhrawardy which aimed to contest elections in the legislative council and acquire greater self-government for Indians, brought out the newspaper *Forward*, later renamed as *Liberty* to fight the

British Raj, aggressively advocated the use of khadi and also emerged as a distinguished Bengali poet.

His real moment of fame came in 1908 when he skilfully defended Ghose in the Alipore Bomb case. As a lawyer, Das had in fact defended several other Indians who had been accused of sedition like Brahmabandhab Upadhyay and Bhupendranath Datta.

After Das passed away in 1925 at the age of 55, his legacy was carried forward by his disciple Netaji Subhas Chandra Bose.

In order to make a democratic choice of name for their neighbourhood, the EPDP association called for a referendum and put 'Purbanchal' and 'Chittaranjan Park' to vote. The result was that the majority of the members voted for the former.

But the new neighbourhood was not named Purbanchal because of the last-minute intervention of the central government. Those who were not happy about the name Purbanchal approached ministers in the Indira Gandhi-led government. Given that Das was a celebrated member of the Congress party at the heyday of his political career and became its leader in 1922, the central government was more than happy to step in to engrave his name upon 'Bangali colony'. Soon after, fliers were distributed among the residents making official the name of their neighbourhood as Chittaranjan Park.

Over the years, residents of CR Park embraced the name as being representative of their Bengali identity as well as their pride in the history of the freedom struggle.

Paritosh was one of those who had voted for Purbanchal but did not mind when eventually the name of Das was chosen. 'Chittaranjan Das was such a great man. He made so many sacrifices for this country and was the one who saved Aurobindo,' he told me.

Ranajit, who had also preferred Purbanchal, told me that initially he was in fact in favour of Netaji's name. 'But Das was the political guru of Bose. That means he was higher than Netaji,' he recalled.

Eighty-two-year-old Arun Guha, a resident of E block in CR Park and the current general-secretary of the EPDP association told me that the choice of Das's name also seemed appropriate to the residents since his legacy had not been given the same kind of visibility as many other heroes of the nationalist movement from Bengal. 'There are so many localities in Delhi itself named after Bengali leaders. But there were none on Chittaranjan Das even though he was such a great man,' he explained.

When geography and history interact with each other, names of places are produced in the process. Perminder Singh in the book, *Celebrating Delhi*, quotes historian Narayani Gupta as she explains this most wonderfully: 'Place names have a meaning in the language and in local history and are part of the cultural fabric of the city.'[21] Indeed, that is what explains why in popular conversations among residents of Delhi, CR Park is still referred to as 'Bangali colony'.

But the popular history of any city is more often

than not overshadowed by the past that the government wants us to remember. The history of the nationalist movement is what shapes the identity of every Indian. Starting from the history textbooks that we memorized meticulously in school, the films we watched, the stories we heard from our grandparents, to the streets we walked on, everything carried a bit of the freedom struggle in it.

Chittaranjan Park was also part of the same process in reinforcing the memory of the fight against the British Raj. Perhaps we can then assume that in the recent naming of institutions and places after stalwarts like Deendayal Upadhyaya and Syama Prasad Mookerjee, a different chapter of Indian history is now being written.

Pamposh Enclave

A new home for a lotus from Kashmir

'Your life will be incomplete if you do not visit Kashmir. It is like heaven,' Jai Kishori Pandit told me over a cup of steaming *kahwa* (Kashmiri tea), seated in her home at Pamposh Enclave. 'One does not have to make an effort to make Kashmir green and beautiful. It is gifted with running streams, tall green trees, bright colourful flowers and a lot more.' Jai Kishori's description of her home in Srinagar was evocative and brimming with nostalgia. For the last three decades though, her home has been shifted miles away and nestled into a little corner of South Delhi.

There is an old, popular saying in Kashmiri, '*Lembi munz pamposh*'. It roughly translates to, when caught in dirt, rise above it all and bloom like a lotus (*pamposh*). Kashmir, they say, is 'paradise on earth', strewn across with tall magnificent mountains, lovely blue lakes, radiant Chinars and of course, the tranquil lotus that blooms in all elegance throughout the valley and has a special place in the hearts and lives of those who inhabit it.

It is the same kind of elegance with which the Pamposh sits on the outer ring road of Delhi, silently, speaking almost nothing of the disturbed stories of severance and longing that ache the hearts of those who have made this neighbourhood their home.

Despite having a decade-long association with Delhi, most of which has been spent residing at areas around Pamposh Enclave, I had never quite known this quaint little locality as anything more than an extension of the posh and upmarket Greater Kailash. The linguistic strangeness of its name had often amused me though. It sounds nothing like the names commonly heard and seen on the streets of Delhi. Neither did it sit in well with the medieval nomenclatures of 'Nizamuddin', 'Chirag Dilli', 'Yusuf Sarai', nor was it part of the stock of names meant for the Hindu mythology aficionados like 'Saket' and 'Greater Kailash'. Neither did it signify the futuristic thinking urbane Delhi, nor was it celebrating the heroes of the nationalist past. For that matter, 'pamposh', to most, would appear as nothing more than a chic sounding combination of two syllables.

The Kashmiri origins of the neighbourhood's name is something I discovered recently, much like the way I came upon the fact that its residents were a quiet group of Kashmiri Pandits. Pamposh, meaning lotus in Kashmiri, is the name that this particular migrant community had enshrined upon their new home in Delhi, when they built it with the hope of a brighter life in the capital, back in the 1960s.

'It was a unanimous decision, you see. Not one person questioned it. "Pamposh" was most fitting,' B.L. Pandit, who is the husband of Jai Kishori, had explained to me while describing the making of Pamposh Enclave.

The lotus, as I learned, has a special place in the Kashmiri way of life. To begin with, it grows in abundance across the multiple lakes in the valley, thereby becoming an essential part of Kashmiri scenery. Its stem, locally known as *nadroo* is a favourite food item, frequently cooked along with mutton, lentils, potatoes and greens. The lotus seeds too, are consumed widely, both for its medicinal properties and their usage in religious ceremonies.

Most importantly though, the Kashmiri Pandits' affinity towards the lotus lies in its religious symbolism. It is believed to be the seat of Goddess Lakshmi and is an important component at every auspicious ceremony. The promising lotus or pamposh is in fact a common favourite name for Kashmiri Pandit children.

The story of this neighbourhood's creation follows the usual narrative of a migrant community finding a place, and in turn, voice for itself in the capital. In the aftermath of the Partition of the country, a decent number of Kashmiri Pandits had settled in Delhi and they decided to approach the government to ask for some land on which they could build a new home. Among themselves, they formed the Kashmiri Cooperative Housing Society for the purpose.

While a majority of those part of this society were Kashmiri Pandits settled in Delhi, there were also those in Kashmir, who, keeping in mind an uncertain future in the valley, registered themselves as part of the society to be shareholders in the land allotted to them.

The group reached out to the Delhi Development Authority (DDA), and in 1963, the village Bahapur was cleared to make way for a colony to house the Kashmiri Pandits. In 1969 the residents of the colony decided on the name 'pamposh' unanimously, and so it came to be

Delhi's only neighbourhood with a majority Kashmiri Pandit population.

In simplistic terms, the naming of Pamposh Enclave would appear to be a product of collective nostalgia of a community, longing to be identified with everything that carried a semblance of home. However, certain aspects of the naming of Pamposh are of interest in reflecting over the unique space that the Pandit diaspora was carving out for itself within the crevices of the national capital.

To begin with, while in popular imagination, the Pandit exodus from Kashmir is widely perceived to have taken place in the 1990s, this colony that came into existence in the 1960s offers a fresh insight into the way in which migration had over centuries become a principal part of the Pandit way of life and can, in fact, be said to be an essential detail in Pandit identity.

Equally interesting is the way in which the Kashmiri Pandit community desired to express its nostalgia. It is worth noting that in the years immediately following the Independence of the country, the spirit of nationalism was still fresh in the social mindset of the capital and the refugees it was making space for. This spirit of nationalist thought manifested itself in the form of neighbourhoods named after heroes of the freedom movement—Lajpat Nagar (named after Lala Lajpat Rai), Malviya Nagar (named after Madan Mohan Malviya) or Chittaranjan Park. There is an interesting correlation that can be observed between newly formed migrant neighbourhoods in post-Independence Delhi, and glorification of nationalist and cultural heroes in their naming.

Pamposh Enclave, in that sense, stands out in its decision to pay homage to a symbol of Kashmiri landscape and Hindu piety. The names of inner lanes, community centres or restaurants at Pamposh too, are striking in the complete absence of cultural or political heroes that might be of importance among the Kashmiri Pandits.

The making of Pamposh is truly one of a community with a unique and long history of migration, the grievances they have learnt to deal with, and most specifically, the lingering memory of home.

For Jai Kishori, it all began when her neighbour whom she fondly called Sherbhai suddenly turned cold, ignoring her routine greetings. 'It was quite strange. Sherbhai was very fond of me. He would call me didi (sister) and ask about my whereabouts every time he saw me,' said Jai Kishori, recalling those days of the 1990s when she first sensed trouble at her doorstep.

It had been brewing for a while though. A Hindu monarch ruling over a substantially Muslim population had given rise to multiple socio-political divides and grievances.[1] The challenges had been kept muted for decades, before the Partition of the Indian subcontinent laid them bare. By August 1947, when over 500 princely states had made up their minds on joining India or Pakistan, the state of Jammu and Kashmir was yet to decide. A curious invasion of tribesmen from the north-west, and the subsequent military intervention of the Indian Union, sealed the fate of the region as disputed. Four decades later, the part of the state that had acceded to the Indian Union on special conditions, continued to boil under religious tensions.

The elections of 1987 were the first sign of trouble. Muslim political parties in the state complained that the elections were rigged against them. Consequently, several militant groups emerged in the state that wanted independence from the Indian Union. Eventually, the insurgency took an Islamic colour and consequently, resulted in thousands of Kashmiri Pandits being uprooted from their homes.

Jai Kishori was in her 50s at that time. She lived with her husband, daughter and in-laws at Karannagar in Srinagar, and worked as an English professor at the government women's college. A simple, dedicated teacher, her life had revolved around academic activities at her college and bringing up her daughter at home. Until 1990, the only times Jai Kishori stepped out of the Kashmir valley were the annual excursions with her students. 'Never did I think that I would reside anywhere else, other than Srinagar,' she said to me.

I was introduced to Jai Kishori by her husband, B.L. Pandit, who is the president of the Kashmiri

Education Culture and Science society in Delhi. 'You will love talking to my wife. She is well known as one of the finest professors in her university. She will narrate our experience of the 1990s most fittingly,' Pandit had said to me, the pride and love for his wife palpable in his voice.

The issue of Kashmir is a complicated one, and that of the Kashmiri Hindu is far more sensitive. Years of grievance, longing, nostalgia, had built a unique identity among the community. I was aware of the complications at hand. There were questions on religion, antagonisms and loss that had to be asked very carefully and with sensitivity, to be able to arrive at what Pamposh meant to this South Delhi neighbourhood's residents.

Surprisingly though, Jai Kishori appeared far more at peace with her past than what I had imagined. Perhaps over thirty years of painstaking rebuilding of her life had infused a confidence in her to be able to face the bygone years with clinical precision. The grief of loss had not died down for sure, but her ability to deal with it had matured with time.

'You see I have no hard feelings against my own people. Even till date my Muslim students call me and visit me whenever they are in Delhi. It was the outsiders who had created trouble in Kashmir,' she said to me.

With her silver-grey hair loosely tied up in a bun, and round dark-rimmed glasses, Jai Kishori had the characteristic appearance of that professor in college who made an attempt to go beyond the classroom to form a relationship of care and affection with her students. Through the many days that I spent interviewing her, she kept reiterating, 'You are just like my daughter. Feel free to ask me whatever you need to know.'

There was indeed much I wanted to know. The experience of the Kashmiri Pandit exodus is an intriguing chapter in Indian history. Very rarely have we come across it devoid of a biased lens. Either it is swept under the carpet as an uncomfortable truth, or it is used as a pawn to justify communal tendencies of a different kind.

'We never experienced any communal differences while growing up in Kashmir,' said Jai Kishori emphatically. Both her maternal and her marital homes were located in neighbourhoods with large Muslim populations. 'When I got married, the Muslim girls in my neighbourhood spent the entire night singing and dancing at my place. They decorated the street leading up to my house to welcome the groom.'

When Sherbhai stopped acknowledging her greetings, she sensed trouble for the first time. Then there were rumours of Muslim youth being radicalized at mosques in the evenings. Things started getting more tense as they would receive letters of intimidation at their doorsteps. 'They would paint messages all over our walls and doors asking us to leave. Then they would come out in procession raising slogans "convert", "run away", or "get killed", they would say,' recalled Jai Kishori.

Finally, in October 1990, she and her husband

decided to leave for Delhi. The trouble, they strongly believed, was a temporary one. Consequently, they packed some clothes in just two suitcases. At home they stored a large quantity of rice, wheat and oil so that they were well prepared to settle into their regular lives soon after they get back. Thirty years down, the house is gone, the land is vacant and so is any hope of returning to their beloved Srinagar.

The journey to Delhi was a quick two-hour flight away. 'We were hardly carrying any cash. It was just a matter of a few days we thought.' Upon landing, the couple immediately went off to a relative's place to put up for a few days. It might be useful to recount that Delhi, by the 1990s, already had a sizeable Kashmiri Pandit population residing in it. Pamposh Enclave by then had already been established and named, and Jai Kishori and her husband did have a small one-bedroom apartment waiting for them in the colony.

The Pandit couple's home at Pamposh had an interesting history to it. It was built back in the 1960s when the colony was first established. In the period following the Independence of the country, the Kashmiri Pandit population was slowly and steadily moving out of the valley. While the Pandit community in the valley was socially and financially at an advantage over the majority Muslim population, they were smaller in number.[2] The consequent accession of the state to the Indian union on conditions laid down by the first prime minister, Sheikh Abdullah (notified in the Indian constitution as

Article 370), resulted in the Pandit community being at a significant disadvantage in their homeland. 'Right from 1947, there was a feeling among the Kashmiri Pandits that they are not safe in Kashmir anymore. We felt that the conditions were biased against us, and many people from the community started moving out,' said BL Pandit to me.

The national capital was one of the most sought-after destinations for those moving out, owing to both its proximity to the state of Jammu and Kashmir, as well as it being the seat of administrative power. When Pamposh Enclave came to be built, Jai Kishori and B.L. Pandit were still in Srinagar. Their family, though aware of the insecurities being faced by the community, had put their faith in the social atmosphere of friendliness in which they had lived for so long and decided to stay put. It was B.L. Pandit's father, who had thought ahead of time, and decided to invest in a small property at Pamposh.

'When my father confided in me his decision to buy a property in Delhi in '60s, I resisted. Having spent much of my youth away from home at service in the Air Force, I was sure that I wanted to spend my post-retirement years in Srinagar,' recounted B.L. Pandit. However, his father was persistent. Being far-sighted and cautious of the troubled times in their home state, he kept secure the one-bedroom apartment at Pamposh for his two sons and their families. Two decades later, it turned out to be a life-saving boon to the family.

'We had been to Delhi a few times in the past,

but never stayed at the flat in Pamposh. But this time was different. As days went by, the situation kept deteriorating in Srinagar. First my brother-in-law and his wife joined us in Delhi and then my parents-in-law,' said Jai Kishori, recalling those days when close to seven or eight members of her family were packed into the one-bedroom flat at Pamposh.

Five decades of life had been uprooted at the flick of a switch, and had to be meticulously rearranged again, that too in a land far away from the lakes and Chinars of Srinagar. For the first few days, Jai Kishori went door to door to each of her relatives' houses, borrowing everything from slippers to utensils. Then there was the issue of cash. Frantically, they reached out to all their friends and well-wishers back in Srinagar, asking them for help in withdrawing their cash from the banks. 'My students were particularly helpful in this regard, and among them too, my Muslim students were the ones who swiftly went about to ensure that money reached us on time,' recounted Jai Kishori.

'We were the lucky ones you see. We had a roof over our heads, however small it may be. There are so many Pandit families who are still living in refugee camps in many parts of the country,' Jai Kishori said. But the couple was soon met with heart-breaking news. A few days after they moved to Delhi, they received a call from their neighbours in Srinagar to let them know that their house had been burnt down by the insurgents.

A few years later, the couple went back to Srinagar to attend a ceremony and paid a visit to the place where their house was situated. Nothing apart from barren land remained. 'It broke my heart. But the worst was yet to come. When I visited our neighbour's house, the same one who informed us about the burning down of our house, I was shocked to see that our carpets and furniture were now decorating their home,' said a straight-faced Jai Kishori. She did not confront them. There was no point, she said. 'That was no longer the place we belonged to.'

'Would you say that in the course of the last 30 years, Pamposh has become home?' I asked the couple. 'Of course not,' Jai Kishori replied swiftly. 'Pamposh is just our attempt to stitch together a life that was uprooted abruptly in Srinagar. Kashmir will always be our home. It is heaven.'

'But why pamposh? What does the lotus symbolize for the Pandits?'

'It is the flower of Goddess Lakshmi and Lord Narayan. It is holy,' replied Jai Kishori. She kept quiet for a few minutes, mulling over the question. 'There are so many childhood memories attached to the lotus. I still dream of those beautiful days when we would go out for picnics in houseboats. We would cook in the boat and eat on the lotus leaf. The flower would be blooming all over the lakes. Pamposh is a symbol of the land that gave birth to us and nurtured us, even when everything and everyone else had turned their backs.'

⁂

Muslim rule in Kashmir is known to have commenced on a favourable and tolerant note in the fourteenth century under Shah Mir's regime.[3] Prior to that, the valley was under Brahmanical and Buddhist regimes. The former governor of Jammu and Kashmir, Jagmohan, who has written a detailed treatise on the history of the state in his book, *My Frozen Turbulence in Kashmir*, notes that Shah Mir 'adopted a humane, enlightened and just approach. He reduced the taxes and treated Hindus and Muslims alike.'[4]

By the end of the fourteenth century though, Islamic rule in the valley turned fanatic under the ruler Sultan Sikandar. Going by the words of Jagmohan, 'It is believed that the Sultan and his chief minister threw into the Dal Lake all the sacred books of the Hindus that they could lay their hands on, and seven maunds of sacred threads of murdered Brahmins were burnt. It is from this period that the predominance of Muslims in the population of the valley begins.'[5]

Since the Independence of the country and more so after the exodus of the Kashmiri Pandits in the 1990s, a narrative of Kashmir's history emerged that has frequently emphasized upon the successive periods of subjugation that Pandits had to undergo in the valley at the hands of Muslim rulers since the time of Sultan Sikander. After a short period of calm following the rule of Sultan Sikander, things turned turbulent in the fifteenth century under the Chaks, who were of Dardic descent and belonged to the Shia sect.[6] Yet again during the rule of the Mughal King Aurangzeb in the seventeenth century, the Pandits were subjected to persecution and the condition worsened under the Afghans in the second half of the century.[7]

Professor of literature Somjyoti Mridha, who has been studying popular representations of the Kashmir conflict, has in an article titled, 'Memories of Home and Persecution: A Study of Kashmiri Pandit Narratives', examined the ways in which history and literature penned down by Kashmiri Pandits was shaped by their experience of exile. 'Pandit narratives published after their exodus from the Kashmir Valley not only describe the socio-cultural consequences of the exile on the members of the community but also ideologically condition their experience of persecution and eviction from the valley,' he notes. Further, he also observes that 'one of the major thematic concerns of all the Pandit narratives is the loss of home.'[8]

Going by Mridha's analysis, the experience of persecution and a longing for a lost homeland are integral aspects that the Pandit community have grown to accept as part of their past and present, and is key to understanding the way they name the spaces they occupied in exile.

One of the several literary works that Mridha analysed in his piece is that of journalist and author Rahul Pandita, *Our Moon Has Blood Clots*. Published in

2013, the book is a memoir in which the author details his personal and collective experience of fleeing the valley in the wake of the insurgency of 1989–90. Though believed to be one of the most poignant and evocative accounts of the Pandit exodus, the book had received mixed reviews. While almost every critic did admire the powerful narrative put together by Pandita, throwing fresh light on the tragic episode, it was also criticized for being selective in its reading of history.

Journalist Anuradha Bhasin Jamwal in her review of the book in the *Economic and Political Weekly* notes that 'Rahul Pandita's book more or less adopts one of the simplified extremes, offering hand-picked memories that are bitter but undeniable. The other problem with the book is that it tends to locate the incidents of 1989–90 within a history that is sifted out to contextualise his sense of victimhood,' writes Jamwal.[9]

Journalist Prayag Akbar, writing in the *Sunday Guardian,* notes that the book is silent about the 'problems faced in those hard years by the Kashmiri Muslim, and reconstructing the history of the state to show the Pandits as a community that has borne a series of historic wrongs.'[10] Akbar also points out Rahul's silence on the issue of 'Kashmiri antipathy towards Dogra rule, and the Pandit complicity in some of the horrors of the time.'

Despite the criticism, Rahul's book is noteworthy in the sense that it provides extremely important insight into the Pandit community's experience of feeling cornered and helpless and the subsequent ways in which they grew to reimagine their past and present.

I reached out to Rahul for an interview on two accounts. One, having witnessed the Pandit exodus from close quarters, his understanding of the community's experience was deeply personal. Secondly, as a journalist with an expertise in conflict zone reportage, Rahul also sees the dispute through a clinical lens. In his over 20 years of journalistic career, Rahul has been associated with media giants in the print and television industry. His work as a war correspondent in Iraq and Sri Lanka, as well as his reportage of the Maoist insurgency in central and eastern India has earned him national and international acclaim.

When I first emailed him requesting an interview, he was busy covering the Hindu-Muslim riots that had gripped North-east Delhi in February 2020. Being one of the few reporters to have written about both the Hindu and Muslim side of the dispute, it earned him both respect and wrath from fellow journalists and the public at large. Understandably, he did take a few days to respond to my request. Being more than happy to discuss with me the Pandit exodus, he asked me to meet with him at the *Open Magazine* office in Panchsheel Park, of which he is currently the deputy editor.

And so, on a pleasant Monday afternoon in March, I met Rahul at his quiet workspace. Having read much about him before the meeting, I expected him to be just as direct and restrained as he was throughout the interview. The only time he gave in to emotions was when he spoke about frequently dreaming of his home in Kashmir.

'I was 14 when I left and I get very panicky when I feel that I am losing memory of home,' he told me as he mentioned dreaming of his home every three or four days, and in brilliant detail. 'It amazes me how it comes to my dream with a certain sharpness and with details I had not noticed before,' he said.

A distinct memory he said he has is that of his father returning home, at 6.00 p.m. sharp, every day. The colour of his father's t-shirt, the look of the door he opened to walk in, the kitchen garden he loved to walk around in and the colourful flowers and trees in the garden, are memories of a long-lost childhood that keep coming back to him regularly, in all its vividness.

'Would you say that this nostalgia for home, and the grief of fleeing from it has been part of Kashmiri Pandit identity even before the exodus of 1989–90?' I asked.

'The idea of migration, or the idea of leaving Kashmir for another place is a part of our collective memory. If you speak to our elders, they will tell you about the seven big exodus that have happened since the fourteenth century,' explained Rahul. He went on to explain how since 1947, there have been several episodes of mini exodus from the valley.

'For example, in the 1960s, many meritorious Kashmiri boys eligible for the engineering and medical colleges there, were told by ministers to leave the seats for the Muslims. It was sort of a veiled threat. It forced many young Kashmiri Pandit boys to leave and look for a life elsewhere,' he narrated, all the while noting names of Pandit doctors and engineers who have done remarkably well in the fields across the world.

Similar waves of migration on account of communal tensions and riots took place in the 1970s and '80s as well. The 1989–90 episode is believed to be the final round of migration.

'But many Pandits and scholars also speak of a peaceful and composite culture of coexistence to be prevalent in the valley before the migration of 1990. Isn't that contradictory to what you say about migration being part of the collective memory of Pandits?' I asked, being curious.

'As a journalist, I record history and over time I have developed a cold, surgical way of looking at things,' said Pandita in his usual straightforward manner. 'A lot of problems in our country have been done due to excessive romanticism. All these things we write in poetry—"the Ganga-Jamuna *tehzeeb*" for instance, is blind to the fact that Hindus and Muslims have been killing each other since ages. In Kashmir's context too, this has done a lot of damage to truth in our country. Because if you keep sugar-coating the bare facts of this country then you would be in trouble.'

He then went on to explain what he understood of one of the most overused words describing Kashmir's culture of coexistence—'*Kashmiriyat*'. You must have come across this word on many occasions. What is Kashmiriyat? It was a word used by a Jammu-based journalist called Balraj Puri in the late 1970s or '80s. Kashmiriyat is nothing but another word for *lihaaz* that exists in any small town or village in India. But how can you believe in Kashmiriyat when you are asking people in the '60s and '70s to leave?'

Speaking about his family's relations with Muslim neighbours, Rahul reflected upon the fact that though there were personal ties, there were also certain unspoken codes of behaviour. For instance, even when his father visited his Muslim friends, and they visited him, it was highly unlikely for them to eat in each other's homes.

'I do not know if we can call it composite culture. But a Pandit living in Kashmir was basically the same as minorities living elsewhere in the world. So basically, you are at the receiving end of anything and everything,' he said.

Rahul then went on to give a few examples. 'For instance, in the 1980s when there was some problem in Jerusalem outside Al-Aqsa Mosque, they started hitting us. When Rajiv Gandhi opened locks of the Ram temple in Ayodhya, they started riots against us. Salman Rushdie wrote a book *The Satanic Verses* that had nothing to do with Kashmiri Pandits, they started hitting us. On 15 August if we did not switch off the lights in our house, they started throwing stones at us. So where is this composite culture we keep talking about?'

'This composite culture exists only till the time we as a minority keep our heads down like a submarine and whenever the tornado hits you, hope that it passes as soon as possible, and when it passes, you behave as if nothing happened. This is the reality of Kashmir.'

Rahul's words were powerful, and indeed crucial in understanding the community's collective experience of being away from home.

'I notice that the Pandit community, having made migration a part of its identity, seeks comfort in motifs from the Kashmiri landscape. Almost every neighbourhood, restaurant, club, etc., established by them across the world is ringing loud with everything that reminds them of their home,' I said to him.

He smiled before answering. 'We are in exile so anything that triggers a memory leads us back to home. Some of these like *samavaar*, *matama*, *pamposh*, *saffron* will come up in any conversation. Especially those motifs that are associated with food. The centrality of our lives in exile is that we cook a lot of food that reminds us of Kashmir. For the Kashmiri diaspora living across the world, food serves as one of the best ways of bonding, considering that many of them have never even been to Kashmir.'

'But what about your heroes? Most migrant communities in Delhi have enshrined names of their heroes in their neighbourhoods. I find it intriguing that the Pandit community is silent about any personality,' I probed further, curious to see his take on what the community thought about their greatest historical figures. 'For instance, Jawaharlal Nehru was one of the key figures from among the community who is noteworthy for his contribution in Indian history.'

Rahul contemplated my question for a while before replying. 'It's a pity that the bitterness of so many years has made us so unforgiving. It is of course a nuisance, but it's also because nobody has listened to their story.'

'This is also a Kashmiri trait, irrespective of whether you are a Hindu or Muslim. I will give an example. When Nehru died, Kashmiri Pandits came out beating their chests. They were saying in Kashmiri, "our beloved father, our eyes have turned blind with sorrow". And if you visit a Kashmiri Pandit function today, they won't even take his name with respect. But that's also true for Kashmiri Muslims. The tallest Muslim leader in Kashmir is Sheikh Muhammad Abdullah. No one has done as much for Kashmiri Muslims as him. When he died in 1982, there were hundreds and thousands of people gathered for his last journey. Just a few years later, he is such a hated figure in Kashmir that his grave has to be guarded all the time since the Kashmiris now want to come and plunder it. Kashmiris have never really recognized their heroes and have been very unforgiving. All we have ever revered are the religious heroes. It is for this reason that they prefer to fall back on motifs that have no controversy attached to them, or are acceptable to all, like "samavaar", "chinar", or "pamposh",' observed Rahul.

'And what is the bitterness about?'

'Bitterness among pandits is that nobody did anything for them, the government failed them, the people, the so called Hindu rashtra failed them, their leaders failed them, their academia failed them, the human rights people failed them,' he answered.

'The Kashmiri Muslims, on the other hand,' he said 'are bitter because they feel that the Indian occupation force does a lot of harm to them. Some people feel that it has become a battle between India and Pakistan and the voice of the Kashmiri does not matter. They also feel that the Kashmiri Pandits have let their story be militarized by the right wing. There are many strands of bitterness.'

Rahul's observation of the Kashmiri personality was intriguing. In this land of never-ending dispute, perhaps it was the bitterness towards history that unified its people. And perhaps for the disgruntled people of Kashmir, history was best forgotten. The only thing that mattered was the memory of home. Pamposh was a manifestation of that nostalgia of the Kashmiri landscape which they carried in their hearts wherever they went, all the while grieving about everything else that was left behind.

Amidst the urban cacophony of South Delhi, Pamposh Enclave would appear to have blended in almost seamlessly with its surroundings. In the architectures of its houses, the planning of its streets, markets and residential blocks, it would appear no different from the neighbouring Greater Kailash 1 and 2. Perhaps the Pandit community has assiduously become a part of Delhi, and made Delhi a part of them. It is only in the name of their neighbourhood, that their identity stands out.

Back in the household of Jai Kishori Pandit and her husband, the couple has been closely following the recent developments in Kashmir. On 15 August 2019, the government of India took the historic decision to revoke Article 370 of the Indian constitution which granted special status and limited autonomy to the state. To curb any protest from the region, all modes of communication, internet and media services were cut off. Thousands of army troops were sent in to quell any kind of uprising. Several top Kashmiri politicians were arrested, including former chief ministers Mehbooba Mufti and Omar Abdullah.[11]

Parts of the Kashmiri Pandit diaspora applauded the move by the Indian government, highlighting the discrimination faced by the Kashmiri minorities on account of the special status.[12] But there were also many Pandits who demanded restoration of Article 370,[13] pointing to the fact that celebrating the revocation is misplaced, vengeful and does nothing to restore legal right and culture of the Kashmiri Pandits.[14]

Jai Kishori and B.L. Pandit observe this all, but comment very little about it. 'Would you like to go back and settle down in Kashmir now or anytime in the future?' I ask. B.L. Pandit was quick to respond. 'Of course not. There is nothing left there for us anymore.'

'No one stood up for us. Neither did the people from our own community do anything to protect us, nor did the government. The government did not even give us refugee status. We are still called migrants, implying that we left our homes out of choice. Truth is that we were forced out,' he said.

'Now we are well settled in Delhi, our children have worked hard and built a bright future for themselves outside Kashmir. What is there for us to go back to in Kashmir?' he asked gulping down the kahwa.

Saket

Modern Delhi's ancient Ayodhya

'We the people of India, having solemnly resolved to constitute India into a sovereign socialist secular democratic republic...'

The birth of independent India was accompanied by a solemn promise to build a country in which the state shall, in all circumstances, observe equality of all religious practices and ideologies. Though as we know, the word 'secular' was added much later in the 1970s when Indira Gandhi's government carried out the infamous 42nd amendment, the founders of modern India were unanimously in support of a constitution that breathed in the spirit of secularism. Independent India was to be modern and democratic, and a secular state was believed to be an essential mark of modernity.

Secularism though, is only one among the several other constituents that make up modernity. Multi-storeyed housing complexes, clean wide boulevards, lush green parks and community centres are few among the many elements believed to be essential in building a space that is considered 'modern'.

A drive across the South Delhi neighbourhood, Saket, is sure to convince one of its modern origins. Quite apart from the chaotic nature of the Old Delhi neighbourhoods, Saket is planned with precision and complemented with all that is necessary for the capital city of a fairly young country to appear aspirational towards the standards of modernity determined by the so called first world countries.

My earliest association with Saket had been for the longest time limited to the cluster of three shopping malls located right opposite Khirki Village collectively known as '*saket wala mall*'. Forever glittering in the decorations of the latest most popular event or festival, the three malls in Saket are an epitome of everything that is rich and aspirational in Delhi.

The malls were of course a product of the new millennium, almost three decades after the neighbourhood was first conceived by the DDA to create a reasonably priced residential space for the middle and upper middle class among the peaking population of Delhi. The activities carried out by the DDA during the 1960s and 70s encompassed clearing out large tracts of agricultural lands, construction of multi storeyed buildings in their place, creation of a lavish sports complex, a multiplex theatre and then much later, three private players built the malls.

Seen from a distance, the development of Saket was not just modern, but also as 'secular' as it could get. It was established by the DDA, an arm of the central government entrusted with the responsibility of providing affordable housing to all residents of Delhi irrespective of their class, caste, religion or any other identity. The DDA shaped up Saket with all kinds of inclusive spaces like a sports complex, malls, etc. Yet, it is interesting that a space that breathes in the spirit of secularism envisioned by the makers of modern India, be named after a popular Hindu mythological site. Saket is the ancient name of the site which is at present known as Ayodhya, popularly believed to be the birth place of Lord Rama.

The name 'Saket' in fact has a rather interesting history. Its association with Ayodhya and the birthplace of Lord Rama is a much later development. The site that is at present known as Ayodhya in Uttar Pradesh, was first identified as Saket in Jain and Buddhist sources dating back to sixth century BCE. The literal meaning of Saket is the place where God resides. It was mentioned in the Pali canon (collection of scriptures in the Theravada Buddhist tradition) as one among the six greatest cities in the country. The city Saketa was also of importance in Jain tradition. It is believed to have been the birthplace of the seven tirthankaras. Whether or not the city's greatness had anything to do with religion, is not clear.

Saket or Saketa was an important centre of urban civilization in India. In the fifth century BCE the city was part of the Kosala kingdom and was under the rule of King Prasenjit. The ruler lived in Sravasti, which was connected to Saket by a main road.[1] The commentary of the Dhammapada (a collection of Buddha's sayings) mentions Saketa to be the place where important public festivals used to be held.[2] Buddha himself is known to have visited the city several times in his lifetime.[3] For that matter, in recent years, there have been a few petitions made by the Buddhist community, asking for the government to declare the site as a Buddha vihara.[4]

As Saket became a flourishing centre of trade, it

was highly coveted by the neighbouring kingdoms of Kashi and Magadha.[5] It was annexed by the Magadha king Ajatashatru and remained part of his empire till its downfall in 200 BCE. Saket also came under the Sungas and the Kushanas, but it was really under the Guptas in the fifth century CE that it reached the zenith of its political importance.[6] It is important to note that historians and archaeologists have frequently debated over whether or not Saket and Ayodhya were the same place.

It is only once we come to the Gupta period that we find a consensus on the fact that Saket and Ayodhya indeed were the same. The process through which that happens tells us much about the way religion and politics interact with each other. When one of the Gupta emperors, Skandagupta, shifted his capital to the site, he is believed to have named it as Ayodhya, possibly as a means to derive religious legitimacy through the ancient epic of Ramayana.[7] To further strengthen the site's connection with the epic, the Gupta king is known to have taken on a title that symbolized his close association with Lord Rama.[8]

Historians also note that under the Guptas, there was a Brahmanical revival in the Gangetic valley, and the Gupta kings emphasized the importance of Ayodhya to legitimize the deification of themselves.[9] In Valmiki's Ramayana, Ayodhya is mentioned as Rama's birthplace. It is also described as having large palaces, wide streets, etc. However, we are yet to come across any archaeological proof to suggest that the present site of Ayodhya was indeed that which is mentioned in the Ramayana.[10]

As anthropologists Reinhard Bernbeck and Susan Pollock note in their essay, 'Ayodhya, Archaeology and Identity': 'The symbolic equation of this place with the mythical Ayodhya is today taken as the factual one.'[11]

In the twenty-first century, the name Ayodhya is well known for its Hindu mythological associations. However, it is also strongly evocative of what remains to be one of the most significant episodes in India's political history, dating back to the 1990s when the Babri Masjid in Ayodhya was demolished by members of a radical Hindu nationalist movement, as a means to reclaim the site for building of a Ram temple.

That the site acquired and planned by the DDA in South Delhi was named Saket is of interest for a number of reasons. First, because Saket gave a certain religious mythological sanctity to a neighbourhood that had been conceived recently for the sake of providing residential space to a new population of the city. The very fact raises some crucial questions as to who the target buyer of the DDA apartments were. Second, Saket unlike Ayodhya, did not carry within it the burdens of a controversial political past. The name struck just the right chords of Hindu sentiments, without reminding them of a more recent disruptive past.

Further, it is also critical to note that the site in South Delhi that is identified as Saket is in fact dotted with a large number of medieval era ruins and villages, most of which date back to a time when the Muslim rulers of the Sultanate dynasty had made the place their capital. Saket was built upon the agricultural lands of mainly two villages in its vicinity—Hauz Rani and Khirki—both of which date back to the Sultanate era and even beyond. While the villages continue to exist in their urbanized form in the fringes, what was once their agricultural land has now been converted into the plush DDA neighbourhood.

While the DDA's conceptualization of the neighbourhood had clearly led to certain class distinctions—pushing one group of people to the fringes and making way for another—there is also an interesting erasure of history that took place in the process. Though the medieval era ruins continue to remind the frequent and infrequent visitor of a glorious Muslim past, it is interesting how the area came to be named after a place most significant in popular Hindu consciousness. There is no better way to understand this dichotomy than by taking a tour of the villages that provided the land for making Saket, and by meeting the people whose collective history lay largely forgotten in providing sanctity to the new-found neighbourhood.

Mohammad Ali is a short, plump man in his early sixties. On most evenings he can be seen chatting with his friends in the Madrasa Zakariya Bahrul-ulum which lies in a tiny corner close to the Saket sports complex. I had first chanced upon him there when I was on my way to look at the sports complex, which was a creation of the DDA in the 1980s. This complex was their attempt to create a modern facility structure for sports enthusiasts in this relatively underdeveloped part of the city.

Ali was born and raised in Hauz Rani, which is presently one among the several areas of Delhi designated as 'urban villages',[12] which are products of Delhi's expansion in the post-Independence era. He identifies himself as a Meo Muslim, majority of whom can be found in the Mewat region of Haryana and Rajasthan. Ethnographic evidence of the Meos suggest that they are a community exhibiting a religious identity which is a unique blend of Hinduism and Islam. Historically, it is believed that they underwent conversion to Islam sometime in the fifteenth century when Firuz Shah Tughlaq was the sultan of Delhi. Some other historians, however, are of the opinion that the Meos came under Islamic influence of certain Sufi pirs much before, from the ninth and tenth centuries.

Unlike the residents of the Muslim quarters of Old Delhi, Ali's speech and tone provides no hint of Urdu influence at all. He believes that his family is descendant of the twelfth century Persian invader Muhammad Ghori whose systematic war of expansion in northern parts of the Indian subcontinent laid the foundation of the Delhi Sultanate which ruled over large parts of the country for the next three centuries. Ali and his family members in fact, continue to use the title 'Ghori' against their names in official records.

In my second meeting with him, Ali took me on a tour of his village which is presently a rather dingy maze of chaotic constructions. He, however, broke out in palpable nostalgia as he spoke with glowing pride about the time when his village was surrounded by large expanses of lush agricultural fields. His most treasured memory is that of playing in a garden in the vicinity of his village which used to be filled with mango trees. The name of the garden, Ali confirmed was 'Bagh-e-Jasrath', but they would popularly refer to it as 'Hauz wala Bagh'.

Both the names, in fact, are of significance in the historicity of the neighbourhood. Jasrath, as many would know, is the mythological king of Ayodhya in the Ramayana, and the father of Rama. Evidence of the presence of a garden in the name of Jasrath was in fact provided by the thirteenth century Chisti order saint, Nizamuddin Auliya.[13] Why a garden by the name of Ayodhya's ruler was present in this area is hard to ascertain, but it is definitely the only possible evidence of a link between the epic Ramayana and the name Saket that was given to the neighbourhood later.

The hauz, or reservoir, which gave the village its name, in fact has a far more fascinating historical significance to the people residing in the area. It is the ruins of this reservoir, in fact, that Ali was most keen on showing me around. As I mentioned earlier, I have been a rather frequent visitor to the plush malls of Saket, but never had I thought of encountering a thick foliage covered hillock being present so close to them, where exist the rocky ruins of this particular reservoir. Walking around this region, one might very well forget that they are inside the premises of New Delhi.

The historicity of this reservoir is hard to determine. No one knows how far back in time it was constructed, or who constructed it in the first place. Nonetheless, it is of immense significance to the residents of Hauz Rani, specifically because it is precisely in the vicinity of this structure that they had established a graveyard where exist several graves dating as far back in time as the fourteenth century when Muhammad Bin Tughlaq had established his capital city Jahanpanah, right adjacent to the reservoir.

Ali showed me around some of the oldest medieval era graves present in the area, and then proudly pointed out to those of his forefathers. All of a sudden, much to my surprise, he whispered a quick prayer near my ears. When I asked him what he was doing, he immediately retorted, '*savdhaan rehna chahiye, shaitan shaktiyan bhi ghumti hain yahaan*' (one must be careful, there might be evil spirits here as well).

It is important to note how this seemingly 'unhistorical' reservoir is of such cultural and religious significance to the community residing in its vicinity. Historian Sunil Kumar has carried out some extensive ethnographic and historical research of the Hauz Rani village. In his book, *The Present in Delhi's Past,* he notes that the Hauz Rani, or the queen's reservoir was constructed sometime in the twelfth century by a queen who is largely missing from the pages of history. The local residents of the village will tell you that this particular queen came from Mehrauli to this reservoir for water. However, there is no substantial historical source to back their claim. What we do know, as Kumar writes, is that the reservoir definitely predated the rule of the Sultanate in Delhi. However, it is only in the fourteenth century that it came to be venerated as a sacred structure by the inhabitants of the region.[14]

'The Hauz-i-Rani was first mentioned in the Persian chronicle of Minhaj-i-Siraj Juzjani (completed in 1260) only because the city constructed by the early sultans of Delhi was in its immediate neighbourhood,' writes Kumar.[15] The plains across the reservoir were in fact frequently used for ceremonial purposes by the Sultan as well. When Muhammad Bin Tughlaq built Jahanpanah, the walls of his new city passed the hauz to its north.[16] Once Jahanpanah was constructed, greater efforts were taken to regulate the flow of water from the Aravalli Hills to the Yamuna. Three streams of water passed by the walls of the hauz, and to control the same, the Satpula dam was constructed to the north-east. The significance of the hauz in the livelihood of the new city drew mostly from the fact that it was related to water, a resource which was both scarce and prized by the medieval monarchs of Delhi.

By the fourteenth century, yet another episode provided a newfound religious significance to the hauz. It was believed that Nizamuddin Auliya received wisdom from Allah while he was praying near the hauz. His spiritual successor Nasir al-Din Chiragh, on the other hand, claimed that the water in the hauz contained special merit.[17]

The significance and structure of the hauz began to deteriorate from the sixteenth century onwards, as the capitals of the early sultans of Delhi underwent a palpable decline and the focal point of the city shifted north during the reign of Shah Jahan. While the reservoir was no longer of economic or cultural significance to the residents of the area, by the nineteenth century, a village came to be built right next to its ruins which continues to be known by the name Hauz Rani. At the same time, the vicinity of the reservoir came to be used as a graveyard by the residents of the village, giving the hauz a new identity.

'This place was so beautiful before the DDA acquired it,' said Ali reminiscing about his childhood days. 'We would grow all kinds of crops here including wheat, ground nuts, bajra. Now all of this is gone,' he added shaking his head.

I was curious to know what he thought of the upmarket neighbourhood that has now replaced the rustic landscape of his childhood home. When I asked him about whether he knew what the name Saket meant, he replied saying it is a popular book, referring to the poetry written by the renowned Hindi poet Maithili Sharan Gupt. When I told him that Saket also is the name of Ayodhya, he shrugged nonchalantly. 'We have no say in it. The government had acquired this land, so they were free to name it whatever they wished. But the government should have preserved the culture of this place. Saket has no relation to this place. The Tughlaqs built this place. So they should have also named it after them. *Is jagah ko aisa hi naam dena chahiye tha jo logon ko yahaan ka itihaas darshaata rahe* (this place should have been named in a way that it reflected its history),' added Ali thoughtfully.

The Hauz Rani village seamlessly merges into yet another urban village that gave up large portions of its agricultural land for the construction of Saket. The Khirki Village is equally haphazard in its nature of urban development. In stark contrast to Hauz Rani, Khirki has no trace of Muslim habitation. On the contrary, it is predominated by Hindu upper-castes, particularly the Chauhans who claim that their ancestors had moved to the village from Indore and Ujjain about 900 years back.[18]

To a first timer, however, the striking aspect of the 'urban village' would probably be the significantly large youth population in it. With a number of rather reasonably priced paying guest accommodations having sprouted all across the area, Khirki is quite popular among the students and young professionals in Delhi. It was also a hub for the Black community in Delhi, who have for the past few years been avoiding the place on account of repeated cases of racial discrimination.

In recent years in fact, Khirki has made news most frequently for its association with drug trafficking, prostitution and racial attacks, thereby diluting its rich history that can be traced back to the late fourteenth century when a mosque was built here under the rule of Firuz Shah Tughlaq by his wazir, Khan-i-Jahan Jauna Shah.[19] Yet again a remnant of Sultanate history, the construction of the Khirki mosque here is testimony to how important an urban centre this part of Delhi had become under Tughlaq rule.

The importance of the mosque in the collective historical consciousness of the community that dwells here is evident from the fact that it is indeed the very structure that lends its name to the rural settlement that sprung up around it, almost at the same time as its construction. The feature that sets Khirki apart from most other mosques in the country is the fact that it is almost completely covered. What probably gives the structure and from there on the settlement around it its name is the grid-patterned set of windows (khirki), resembling the jharokhas which are common in Rajasthani architecture pierced on its three sides.[20]

At present, the mosque stands tall at the centre of the

village, but hidden from public view by the chaotic urban construction and foliage that surrounds it. Surprisingly though, the residents of Khirki do not even recognize it to be a mosque. Rather, they refer to it as a *quila* or fort and ascribe to it a history, very different from that which historical records suggest.

I had chanced upon Mahinder Kaushik during a leisurely tour of the settlement. I was casually discussing my attempt to understand Khirki's past, when he invited me over to his place. Hardly did I expect being led to a large, swanky apartment, designed in the most luxurious way, in stark contrast to the external appearance of the urban village. The rustic past of Khirki, however, is deeply embedded in the memory and consciousness of both Mahinder and his wife who continue to refer to the place as 'gaon' (village) and their neighbours as 'gaonwale' (villagers). 'This was a village actually. We had cows at our home, we would have to go far away to get water from the well,' said Kaushik. He added that the space where the malls have come up and the Saket district court is present was in fact their agricultural fields. 'It was filled with all kinds of agricultural produce including pulses, vegetables, etc., when the government decided to acquire it. They ran a bulldozer over their fields. The farmers were very sad, but what could they have done? The area came under the masterplan of the DDA,' remembered his wife, Samita Kaushik.

When I started asking him about the mosque located next to his house, he cut me short and immediately corrected me. 'This was never a mosque, it was a quila,' he said with a passionate surety in his eyes. When I probed further, stating that it is well known as the 'Khirki masjid' he reclined back stating, 'This came to be considered as a mosque because the Mohomeddans were ruling here. *Unka shasan tha toh woh jo chahe karenge* (it was their rule so they could do whatever they wished).'

'So who constructed this "quila"?' I asked him. 'Prithviraj Chauhan had built this fort, and the entire village community used to live inside it,' he replied. Popular narratives in Delhi, often believe that the twelfth century Chahamana dynasty monarch Prithviraj Chauhan had built his capital in Qila Rai Pithora, which is a fortified complex in Mehrauli. The residents of Khirki frequently associate their settlement's history with that of Chauhan's rule in large parts of north-west India, including Rajasthan, Haryana and Delhi. However, historical records are at odds with the popular narratives.

Texts that were contemporary or near-contemporary to the Chauhan ruler, place his capital to be in Ajmer.[21] No concrete historical evidence is available to connect him with Delhi. Chauhan's governor, Govind Rai had his small fort, called Lal Kot near Mehrauli.[22] Medieval texts associated Prithviraj Chauhan with Delhi, more as a means of connecting the city to an important political lineage.[23] The Hindu upper-caste residents of Khirki Village have retained this association, collectively remembering Chauhan to be their historical predecessor.

For the past couple of years, the residents of the village have been regularly petitioning the government to change the name of the mosque to 'khirki quila'. The issue began when in June 2015, some people forcefully entered the monument to offer prayers within its premises, leading to conflict with the local residents.[24] The matter was brought to the notice of the local police who immediately brought the situation under control. Soon after, the Residents Welfare Association (RWA) of Khirki Village wrote to the government to officially prohibit the offering of prayer inside the monument.

Two days later, the Archaeological Survey of India (ASI) directed the Commissioner of Police (South) to look into the matter and ensure that 'there is no violation of the Ancient Monument and Archaeological Site and Remains Act, 1958, Rules 1959, and Ancient Monument and Archaeological Site and Remains (amendment and validation) Act 2010, and from law and order angle.'

While offering of prayers came to be prohibited in accordance with government rules regarding preservation of archaeological sites, the residents of the village have ever since been demanding the removal of the suffix 'mosque' against the monument. K.C. Rana (80), who has spent all his life in Khirki Village and is presently the secretary of the Khirki RWA, spoke with me at length on their demand. 'Never in all these years have I seen *namaaz* (Islamic ritual of daily prayer) being offered here. Then how can we call this a mosque?' he asked thumping the desk next to him. He went on to show me all the letters he has written to the government in the last four years and the response he has received. 'The ASI has been telling me that this is a protected monument and is known to be a mosque in their records,' he said showing me the letter from the ASI. 'However, please tell me if the government can change the name of the Mughal Sarai station to Pandit Deendayal Upadhyaya junction, if the name of Aurangzeb Road can be changed, if so many other names can be altered, then what is their problem with changing the name of this mosque to Khirki Quila?'

When I explained to him the fact that all historical records suggest that this indeed is a mosque, Rana rigorously shook his head. 'Indian history is very convoluted. When Muslim rulers took over Delhi, they wrote the history of this city from their perspective. They wrote that this is a mosque, but we the residents here believe that this is a fort. Now, who is to say what is authentic?' he asked.

The idea of religious plurality in India has always been its most unique feature. However, it also hits a raw nerve, instigating some of the strongest disputes, both in the popular narratives of the people of this country, and in the corridors of administrative power. Which community came before whom, whose religious ideas have a longer historical trajectory, whose history should predominate over others', these are the questions that the country has been grappling with since its very inception.

Before taking my leave, I asked Rana about his take on the name of the urban space which now makes up his agricultural land. 'Saket is a beautiful name. I know it has something to do with ancient mythology,' he said with a broad smile on his face. When I pursued further, asking what about the fact that the area is dotted with Delhi's Islamic past, he quickly interrupted me. 'How many times should I tell you? This was a Hindu area. Muslim rulers converted everyone. Now should the Hindu inhabitants not name the place as per their wish?'

❋

The newest occupants of the land adjoining the Khirki masjid and Hauz Rani are the buyers of the property built by the DDA. The DDA, which was created in 1957 with the objective of ensuring a structured development of the city, has played a significant and interesting role in the history of Delhi.

The central government agency was formed in the wake of the Partition when close to half a million refugees moved into the city within a single year. Between 1947 and 1951, the city's population is believed to have risen from 7 lakhs to 17 lakhs.[25] In the absence of adequate space, the new inhabitants of the city occupied any and every bit of land available in the southern, western and eastern regions which were far beyond the city limits.

The predecessor of the DDA, the Delhi Improvement Trust (DIT) had come into being in 1941 on the recommendation of Arthur Parke Hume to manage urban congestion in the city, post the shift of the capital from Calcutta. Less than a decade later, the DIT was considered inadequate in its capacity to take care of the capital which was expanding rapidly as well as haphazardly.

For a city that had, for the longest time, been functioning within a network of multiple levels of intertwined governance, the DDA had an overarching role to play, not just in terms of planning land use patterns and housing for the city, but also in terms of the power it exerted on 'encroached' land and the jhuggi-jhopdi clusters which had cropped up. Examining the number of commercial, recreational and housing spaces directly controlled by the DDA presently, one can safely say that the authority literally built the newest of the city of seven cities.

The authority started working through its master plans since 1962, with the objective of bringing in more and more land under its control so as to develop them for residential purpose. Further, in 1967 they started with their housing projects which consisted of building large scale residential neighbourhoods with basic amenities like electricity, water, commercial spaces, etc. Since then, they have been periodically working on these projects every few years. These housing schemes are meant for four categories of aspirants—high income groups (HIG) middle income groups (MIG), low income groups (LIG) and Economically Weaker Sections (EWS).

The process of allotting property on the part of the DDA is as follows. First, the project is made public through various newspapers. Aspirants apply for an apartment with an application fee. Then a public draw takes place and those whose names get picked are allotted property. The biggest housing builders of New Delhi used to see applications pouring in bulk for their flats. Somehow in recent years, the same authority is seeing a sharp drop in aspirants for their projects.[26]

While the recent drop in applications have been attributed to the fact that their newest projects are in outer Delhi, an area not so much aspired by the young professionals in the city, the DDA's overall housing schemes have been severely criticized in the past for not being able to meet with the goal of inclusive development that had been promised. A 2014 report published by the Centre for Policy Research (CPR) titled 'The Delhi Development Authority: Accumulation Without Development', had detailed out the ways in which the central government agency has largely benefitted the higher income groups, leaving behind large parts of Delhi's population.[27]

As observed by the report, the DDA emerges as 'an organisation that is at once relatively efficient and successful at certain tasks—like acquiring land and providing high end amenities—and extremely slow to accomplish others—like building and allotting low-income housing.' Consequently, the implications of it is such that 'the city's poorest residents become squatters as the DDA acquires the land on which they live, yet they have few affordable housing options.'

The class distinctions between those whose land has been acquired to build a modern residential neighbourhood and those who consequently live in the newly built up area is quite evident in the case of Saket. While the 13 blocks of DDA housing in Saket are clearly populated by middle and upper-middle class individuals who were mostly working in government and private sector jobs when they bought the apartments, the urban villages of Hauz Rani and Khirki on the other side are far from acquiring the financial and social status being enjoyed by the former.

Equally interesting is the religious distribution among the occupants of the DDA flats and that of the villages on whose land it is built. Among the multi-storey buildings and wide tree-lined boulevards of Saket, it is hard to come across any resident who is visibly from a minority community, except for a few Sikhs. The absence of Muslims among the residents is rather odd, considering the fact that there are multiple mosques and a madrasa in the area, as well as the fact that the adjoining Hauz Rani is teeming with a majority of those belonging to the Islamic faith.

It is worth noting that when the first master plan of Delhi was furnished by the DDA in 1962, Saket was mentioned nowhere in it. The neighbourhood developed nearest to it was the refugee settlement named after the notable freedom fighter, Madan Mohan Malviya—Malviya Nagar. When the neighbourhood did get established in the early '70s, it was still not referred to as Saket. Rather, it was seen to be an add-on to Malviya Nagar, and was named as Malviya Nagar Extension.

The first time that the area made an appearance as Saket was in 1977 when the DDA came out with the self-financing scheme for its buyers. The brochure clearly mentioned that 'the flats now being offered are distributed in four different blocks in Malviya Nagar Extension, which has been renamed as "Saket".'

The story of how and why the name change took place is a difficult one to piece together. Anyone who is even minutely aware of the functioning of the DDA would be able to tell of the tedious bureaucracy that it can put one through. As a journalist covering Delhi, I have often found myself exhausted, on the verge of despair, having to beg officials from the authority to have a word with or get a quote from. While my journalistic inquisitions have most often been based on everyday affairs, the question about how one of their neighbourhoods came to be named some 40 years back was one of complete surprise to anyone I spoke to from the DDA.

In almost every case, and no matter which department I spoke to, I was politely and sometimes rather rudely directed to some other office or officer. In a lot of cases, I was clearly told that the answer to my rather unnecessary question lies buried underneath piles of official files and the dust accumulated on them through the years of being ignored.

However, my conversation with a certain retired officer had made a few things clear for me. The name of the gentleman cannot be revealed because as explained earlier, getting a DDA official on record is one of the hardest things I have had to do as a journalist. However, this gentleman whom I had very unkindly woken up from his afternoon siesta on a sultry summer day with my phone call, was gracious enough to brief me on the way the DDA works when it comes to naming the colonies it puts together.

'Things are very informal in cases like these, you see. Say in the case of Dwarka, we were asked what name would suit the area. We suggested this name since we thought that anything from Indian mythology would sell well. There was not much thought put into this,' he explained. The residential neighbourhood in south-west Delhi, named after the mythological city where Lord Krishna is believed to have settled, was also built by the DDA, and continues to be developed as a 'smart city' project. As explained by the gentleman, the origins of Saket must also have been somewhat similar. While Saket is no 'smart city', it definitely appears as one of the more ambitious projects of the DDA.

During one of my multiple visits to the neighbourhood, I had come across Sanjeev Kohli, a member of the Saket H block RWA. Now in his 80s, and previously a marketing professional, Kohli was one of the first buyers of the flats in the 1970s. Kohli vaguely recalls the naming of Saket in the following way. One bright afternoon, sometime in the late '70s, the residents of the still new colony met at M block to discuss the everyday affairs and functioning of the neighbourhood. This meeting was presided over by a certain politician and member of Parliament who had also bought a plot in M block. The residents were asked to give their opinion on the proposal to change the name of the neighbourhood to Saket to give it an identity distinct from Malviya Nagar, and it was immediately accepted since it was considered a 'beautiful name'. 'All of this happened in a very casual way,' said Sanjeev.

The recent land pooling policy launched by the DDA in 2019 aims to provide 17 lakh houses in the capital, including 5 lakh for those belonging to the EWS.[28] As part of their program, the central government body has introduced a portal on their website asking citizens to suggest names for five new urban extensions which will be developed as sub cities.[29]

The *Hindustan Times* report informing the public of the initiative quotes the DDA Vice Chairman Tarun Kapoor saying 'We want people to feel part of the new development [...] The shortlisted names will be presented at a high-level meeting chaired by the lieutenant-governor where the final decision will be taken.'[30]

The same report also notes that in their previous

initiatives of housing developments, the DDA has often finalized a name depending upon what they thought would be most relatable to the citizens and then asked the residents for their comments on it before finalizing it. This was the case with Dwarka, Narela (named after a nearby village) and Rohini (named after the series of satellites launched by the Indian Space Research Organisation in 1979). One can only guess that a similar development would have taken place in the case of Saket as well.

Whatever be the precise development of the process through which Saket was named, one can be sure about the fact that a subconscious religious identity determined to a large extent, the way a majoritarian government and the religious group that forms its majority population, came together to name one of its many residential projects. Of course, one can argue that the DDA had no such intention of imposing majoritarian sentiments. No doubt, despite the name of the colony, fact still remains that religion in no way features in the wide range of modern developments that the authority ensured there, thereby keeping up with the ideals of 'secularism' that new India dreamt of.

However, one has to consider the fact that imposition of religious notions need not always be a bold and conspicuous attempt, the way the demand for the Ram temple in Ayodhya has been ongoing since the 1990s. Saket in no way makes a political statement. Neither does it contain within it references to a history of communitarian battles, but does indicate the belief system of its residents. It would be interesting to examine if the DDA in its ongoing attempt to involve citizens in naming its new sub-cities, finalizes even one which is connected to the Islamic, Christian or any other faith that threads India together in the vivacious spirit of diversity.

Shaheen Bagh

A safe haven for the political Muslim

WE THE PEOPLE OF INDIA
REPUBLIC
इश्क इन्क्लाब
मोहब्बत जिंदाबाद
CONSTITUTION OF INDIA
Fearless
SHAHEEN BAGH

When I met Bilkis Bano for the first time, it had been just over a month since she was honoured by *Time* magazine as one among the hundred most influential people in the world. Less than a year ago, she, along with thousands of women like her, occupied 150 metres of an arterial road connecting Delhi to Noida in Uttar Pradesh. Shaheen Bagh was their site of protest and Shaheen Bagh was also a moment loaded with historical significance. Their demand? The repeal of a law passed by the Indian government which they feared might result in a large number of Muslims losing citizenship.

The protest had died down by then. But Bilkis's name was all over the press as being the face of the women who challenged the Indian government on a most controversial law. She lived in a small one-bedroom apartment in a narrow, congested lane of the neighbourhood with her son, daughter-in-law and granddaughter. When I called her son to arrange an interview with her, he informed me of the many calls he keeps getting with similar requests. But he was more than happy to have his mother speak with me.

When I reached their home for the interview, Bilkis was sitting cross-legged in one corner of the brown carpeted floor of her living room. Her round, kohl-lined eyes were the first to catch my notice. They glittered with a kind of fiery spirit unlike anything I had seen before. For an 82 year old, Bilkis was unusually agile. She quickly arranged for a cup of tea for me before sitting down again for our conversation.

From December to March, Bilkis along with the many women who are popularly called the 'dadis of Shaheen Bagh', sat through biting cold, powerful rain and many a threat to their lives, as they demanded justice for their community. The sudden emergence of a global pandemic abruptly stopped their protest before the Citizenship Amendment Act (CAA) could be repealed, but the movement created by these women would indeed go down in the pages of history.

The CAA is a piece of legislation passed by the Indian Parliament on 11 December 2019. It asserts to provide citizenship to all non-Muslim persecuted religious minorities from Afghanistan, Bangladesh and Pakistan. Critics of the CAA argue that the legislation in combination with the nationwide National Register for Citizens promised by the home minister could render many Muslims who are unable to provide adequate birth or identity requirements stateless.[1]

I asked Bilkis how she felt about being honoured by *Time* magazine. 'It felt good, but I am a bit sad as well,' came her prompt response, almost as if she had expected my question and had kept the answer well practised beforehand. 'Why sad?' I asked. 'We could not complete the work for which we had set out.'

Bilkis had a tall, slender frame. She wore a salmon-coloured chikankari salwar kameez, her head covered with a dupatta. Strong lines of wrinkles covered her face and a tiny gold nose pin stood out as the only piece of jewellery she wore.

She said that this was the first time she had participated in something like this. Her son, who sat beside her beaming with pride, informed me that his mother was largely unlettered, having only received some education on the Quran in her childhood. In all these years, she had never stepped out of the roles expected of her as a wife, mother and grandmother. 'But my mother is the most informed member of our house, spending hours watching the news on television,' said Mansoor with a wide grin on his face.

They both sat cross-legged on the carpeted floor of the hall in their two-roomed flat. Mansoor came to Delhi in the early 1990s and currently earns a living as a translator for the Arabs visiting India for medical treatment. For the past few months though, business had been rough owing to restrictions on international travel due to coronavirus. Mansoor's wife was busy in the kitchen as his seven-year-old daughter sat on his lap, playing with my phone and purse. 'Do you like going to school?' I asked. 'No,' she said, blushing. 'What do you want to do once you grow up?' 'Be a doctor,' came her prompt reply as she looked at her father and smiled.

On being asked what prompted her to initiate the protest, Bilkis replied assertively, 'They were beating up young boys and girls in Jamia. If the youth is being threatened this way, then how will they grow and how will the country progress?'

The incident she was referring to took place on

15 December 2019, when a violent confrontation took place between the students of Jamia Millia Islamia who were protesting against the CAA and the Delhi police. The following day's newspapers reported at length and with disturbing details on how the police had entered the library and attacked the students studying there.[2] Bilkis and her son say that it was this incident that forced the women to step out of their homes. 'This government feels that we do not understand anything. For all these years I have taken care of my home and children efficiently. If I can do so much, then I can understand everything happening around me as well,' said Bilkis.

Within days, the leaderless sit-in at Shaheen Bagh had turned from being a mere act of resistance against police brutality in Jamia to a historic movement with Muslim women becoming the face of it. Soon after, inspired by the 'dadis of Shaheen Bagh', many similar gatherings of burqa-clad women broke out in other parts of Delhi and India. However, we do know that years from now, when a history of the anti-CAA movement will be written down, it is Shaheen Bagh that would become the centre of it all.

There are many ways in which Shaheen Bagh stood out as the focal point of what can easily be described as the biggest political struggle carried out by the Muslim community in India following Independence. To begin with, it broke many a stereotype about Muslim women being subdued, voiceless beings, often at the mercy of the men in their households. Here they were carving out an identity and space for themselves. Moreover, it was not just any identity, rather a political one.

Politics, that domain which is almost everywhere exclusively understood as male dominated, was being occupied by a group of Muslim women, a majority of whom had never left the thresholds of their homes before.

The movement did one other thing. It put upon the map of the city, this little neighbourhood of south-east Delhi whose existence was almost unknown to many Delhi residents. In the next four months, Shaheen Bagh had become a household name across the country and had soon found itself covered extensively by international media.

Of the many Muslim neighbourhoods in Delhi, why is it that Shaheen Bagh became the face of the political struggle of Muslims in India? Delhi has, for centuries, shared an intimate relationship with Muslims. From the twelfth century onwards, it had served as the capital for successive Muslim dynasties. Subsequently, the city had carved out a distinctly Islamic character for itself. Even though the 1857 movement, the Partition and the outbreaks of religious riots in India had disturbed the Muslim demographics of the city, there continues to remain large pockets of Delhi which are characteristically Muslim. For that matter, out of Delhi's nine districts, four have a substantially high Muslim population—north-east, south, central and north.[3] Areas like Nizamuddin West, Old Delhi, Seelampur, Mustafabad, Hauz Rani and many others have a large population of Muslims. Yet, what was it that made Shaheen Bagh more political than the rest?

It is indeed the political nature of Shaheen Bagh and its surroundings that made me curious about the story behind its name. *Shaheen* in Persian means a falcon. 'This bird can fly higher than anyone else,' sixty-one-year-old Shariq Ansarullah told me, who had conceived of the neighbourhood in the 1980s and named it. He was inspired, as he told me, by the great poet Muhammad Iqbal, better known as the writer of the song, 'Saare Jahan se Achha'. Iqbal had mentioned the falcon in many of his poems. In particular, it was one poem that had caught his attention.

> *'Tu shaheen hai, parwaz hai kaam tera, tere samne asman aur bhi hain'*
> (You are a falcon, your task is to fly; before you there are other skies as well to cover).[4]

Like Mansoor, Shariq too originally belonged to Uttar Pradesh. Iqbal's words must have meant something to a young Shariq, who had grown up as a Muslim in an India that was still recovering from the bruises caused by the Partition. They must have given him some strength and hope as he set out to draw the colony in one corner of this large, daunting capital city.

The story of his journey from a tiny village in Rampur to Delhi, in pursuit of education and a life of prosperity later, details the lives and aspirations of the residents of Shaheen Bagh and why the neighbourhood's name is of significance.

Who better to tell the story of its birth, than the man himself who bought the land on which Shaheen Bagh stands, and thereafter named it?

The winter of 2019 is hard to forget for any city reporter based in Delhi. The sounds of protest against the CAA were making headlines for days on end. As a reporter for the *Hindustan Times* then, I would visit Shaheen Bagh at least three to four times a week. The energy in the air, reverberating with slogans of *azaadi* was unlike anything one had encountered before. It was in the course of my reporting at Shaheen Bagh that I came across Shariq Ansarullah. A colleague of mine had interviewed him for a story she was doing and was generous enough to share his contact details with me.

I rang up Shariq sometime in early March 2020, when the protest was beginning to subside on account of a raging pandemic and the possibility of a nationwide lockdown. His voice sounded thin and feeble over the phone, even though his eagerness to tell me all about his Shaheen Bagh was well evident. It was a quick five-minute conversation before he asked me to come down the following day to the Shaheen Public School, which he had built in the 1980s while planning the colony.

Having spent the last three months frequently visiting Shaheen Bagh, it took me no time to locate Shariq's school. Unlike the chaotic streets of Old Delhi, Shaheen Bagh was more planned. Rows of flats and shops lined up beside each other. However, it was not organized and definitely in no way opulent. Like any other unauthorized colony of Delhi, Shaheen Bagh too had hanging wires all across its skyline and unpaved, uneven roads, which are a challenge for most pedestrians.

I stepped inside the school to find a large courtyard with corridors and classrooms on all four sides. Classes had been suspended at that time, on account of the pandemic, so an eerie silence prevailed all over. I was met by one of the helpers sweeping the corridors, who asked me why I was there. When I told him that I had an appointment with Shariq, he quickly dropped the broom and walked me down to his office.

As I entered his office, I saw Shariq sitting at his desk. On seeing me, he looked up with a wide toothy grin. 'You are here,' he said, ushering me to take a seat opposite him. He looked tall and slender, with a thick, white beard on his face and a pair of dark square-rimmed glasses on his nose. In his black, high neck, buttoned-up kurta and white pyjamas, he looked like the disciplinarian and yet adoring principal which he perhaps is.

This was the first among a number of meetings I had with Shariq. In the course of those lengthy conversations, he told me all about his life at Rampur and how, as an enthusiastic teenager, he dreamt of a life of prosperity in Delhi. He was 17 when he came to the city to study Arabic honours at Jamia Millia Islamia, following which he did a master's from Jawaharlal Nehru University. His father at that time was a schoolteacher in Rampur. With his meagre earnings, he somehow struggled to bring up Shariq along with five of his siblings.

While he was still a student, Shariq decided to buy a small plot of land to build a house for himself in Abul Fazl Enclave, which lies adjacent to where Shaheen Bagh is today. He borrowed some money from his uncle who lived in Saudi Arabia and made the purchase. 'Mine was one of the only few houses in the area. The rest of the place was covered in thick forests with snakes loitering around. When my relatives visited me from Rampur, they would be shocked to see the condition of the place and ask me why I wanted to live here,' he told me in his soft, wobbly voice.

Shariq's decision to move to Delhi at such a young age and buy a house here was indeed an ambitious one. He was the only one among his siblings as well as among his friends in school who went out of his hometown for the sake of higher education. Like his brothers and sisters, Shariq too had been educated in the Islamic mode of learning at a Madrasa. 'Why did you think of moving to Delhi?' I asked. He replied with a calm voice, 'I had an attraction towards Delhi. People come empty handed to this city but are blessed with every kind of success.'

After completing his master's in 1984, Shariq was left wondering what to do next. That is when he thought that just like the developer who created Abul Fazl Enclave, he too would like to buy the surrounding land and build housing plots on it. Consequently, he met Jaggan Singh, the one who owned the land in Jasola Village where Shaheen Bagh stands. Over the course of five years, Shariq bought 80 bighas of land from him and started selling plots to potential residents. By the end of 1980s, the area had turned into a fully established colony. With the profits that he made, Shariq opened two schools and a mosque in the area. His customers were students of Jamia or other migrants who came in from UP and Bihar. All of them were Muslims.

'Did you intend to make a colony for Muslims?' I asked. 'No, not really,' he said, shrugging his shoulders. 'But it so happened that only Muslims came to live here. Shaheen Bagh has a 100 per cent Muslim population.'

The idea of 'Muslim localities' in Delhi has a long history stretching back to the Partition of the country. At different points in time, different reasons were suggested for creating these small ghettos occupied only by Muslim residents.

But I was curious to know why a newcomer to the city in the 1980s did not aspire to be part of one of the neighbourhoods which was being built by the DDA. As I mentioned in my previous chapter, the DDA had by then established itself as an overarching city planner, with the objective of ensuring a structured growth and development of Delhi. By the late 1970s, the authority was in the process of building several well-planned neighbourhoods across the city. 'Did you ever think of applying to the DDA's housing schemes?' I asked Shariq.

'I did. I had applied to the DDA thrice for their housing schemes in Dwarka and Rohini. A few of my friends too had applied at the same time. None of our names came up in the lottery ever,' said Shariq. He quickly added, 'Somehow Muslims have always been kept separate. You look at the condition of Shaheen Bagh today. I established it in the 1980s, and till now there is no park, bank, hospital, post office or even drinking water facility here yet.'

When it came to deciding a name for the neighbourhood, Shariq first thought of naming it after himself just like the developer Abul Fazl had done with the adjoining colony. But it was his love for Allama Iqbal that presided over all else, and he decided to name it after 'shaheen', a metaphor that was most widely used by the poet.

'This bird, shaheen, can fly very high up in the sky. No other bird can fly like that,' said Shariq describing the aptitude of the metaphor. 'Moreover, shaheen never preys on birds or animals that are weaker than himself. It is a mark of his courage.'

'Iqbal praised this bird a lot in his poems. He encouraged everyone to become like this bird,' he said as he narrated the lines of Iqbal's poem. 'We must aspire to fly higher. We must not restrict ourselves to just one sky. There is a lot more to achieve. This was Iqbal's message to us.'

The words of Iqbal had a powerful impact on Shariq since he was a little boy. He told me how back in his school at Rampur, they would begin the day with a popular Urdu *dua* (prayer) authored by Iqbal titled, 'Lab Pe Aati Hain Dua'. Over the years, he had read almost everything written by the poet, and pondered over them in great detail.

'What is it about Iqbal's writings that touched your heart so much?' I asked.

He thought for a brief while, silently, before answering, 'His commentary on the times he was living in. Iqbal insisted that Muslims were behind everyone else in terms of education. He would write that we need to wake up and move ahead in life.'

A brief comment needs to be made here about who Allama Iqbal was and what his writings conveyed. Scholars of Urdu literature have frequently commented on the fact that Iqbal is easily one of the most controversial figures of South Asian history. He is championed by some as one of the chief founders of Pakistan, while there are others who consider him to be a staunch patriot of India.[5] Both Nehru and Jinnah have in their writings, lent support to the words of Iqbal. His name is appropriated by vastly differing political, religious and social groups. One reason for Iqbal to be appropriated or misappropriated by so many different groups is due to the vast range of issues he was writing about. Some were political, some social, while there were others that were purely philosophical and ethical.

Iqbal was born in 1877 in Sialkot which is now in Pakistan and was most active as a writer in the late nineteenth and early twentieth centuries. He passed away in 1938, by which time he was also politically active. He was an active member of the All India Muslim League. As a politician, he is most remembered for his 1930 presidential address to the Muslim League, in which he expressed his desire for the creation of a Muslim state in India. 'Self-government within the British Empire, or without the British Empire, the formation of a consolidated north-west Indian Muslim State appears to me to be the final destiny of the Muslims, at least of North-West India,' he had said.[6] Consequently, he is often seen as the mind behind the Partition of the country, even though he passed away almost a decade earlier. Nonetheless, in a post-partitioned Indian subcontinent, Iqbal is seen as 'national poet' in Pakistan, while in India, he is identified as a 'Muslim poet'.

'To brand Allama Iqbal as an Islamic poet or writer is the biggest harm done to him. Just like Rabindranath Tagore cannot be called a poet of Bengal, similarly it is unfair to call Iqbal a poet of Islam,' Professor Zahidul Haque had told me over an hour-long conversation over the phone, when I reached out to him for a comment on Iqbal.

Professor Haque teaches Urdu literature at Hyderabad University. When I asked him what Iqbal's writings meant to a Muslim growing up in the 1960s and '70s in India, he told me that at a time when the wounds of Partition were still fresh, it was common for Iqbal to be seen as a poet of Muslims. 'However, in his poetry, Iqbal also showered praises on Guru Nanak and on Lord Rama. Do you know that Iqbal translated the Gayatri Mantra as well?' he asked me.

'But many scholars say that Iqbal in his writings was reminding Muslims of a glorious past. Does that not make him a Muslim poet?' I asked.

'Well yes, he was writing about the glory of an Islamic past. But he also wrote many other things that went completely against Islamic philosophy. For instance, he would often praise *Iblis* or Saturn in his works for being firm in beliefs and being rational. Primarily, he was interested in the awakening of the South Asian people,' he explained, as he went on to list for me some other metaphors regularly used by Iqbal.

The *Mard-i-kamil* or a 'complete human being' or a perfect man was a most favourite one among them, indicating one who is an ideal combination of reason, vision and action. Yet another symbol used by the poet frequently was that of the shaheen or the falcon.

'Nahi tera nasheman Qasr-e-Sultani ke gumbad par
Tu Shaheen hain basera ka pahado ki chattano mein'

These words written by Iqbal in his poem, 'Aik Ke

Naujawan Ke Naam', translates as 'your abode is not the dome of a royal palace, you are a falcon and should live in the rocks of mountains.'

In another poem, titled 'Shaheen' Iqbal wrote,

'Parindon ke duniya ka dervaish hoon main,
Ke Shaheen banata nahin aashiyana'
(I am a dervish in the kingdom of birds, the falcon is not one to build nests).

As Professor Haque explained to me, Iqbal was constantly using the metaphor of the falcon to inspire the younger generation to strive hard and achieve their goals.

But how would someone like Shariq, whose family chose to be in India rather than crossing the religious divide, and one who grew up in an India of the 1960s and '70s, be interpreting Iqbal's words? In Shariq's opinion, Iqbal was truly writing to inspire the Muslim community.

Professor Dayne E. Nix has written in great detail about how Iqbal's writings can be interpreted as an attempt to 'restore Muslim dignity'.[7] Historian Iqbal Singh Sevea, who has also worked extensively on Iqbal's socio-political thought, suggests in his work that 'Iqbal's writings reveal his concerns over Muslim decline and his attempt to chart a path for the regeneration of the community.'[8]

This issue of reviving the spirit of Muslims, motivating the community to reclaim its golden days of a bygone era, was something that many poets from the Islamic community were engaging with in the nineteenth and twentieth centuries. As the Mughal, Ottoman and Safavid empires declined in the eighteenth century, a generation of Islamic reformers emerged who felt the need for Muslims to re-interpret Islam within a declining political context.[9] In an India which was now under the control of the East India Company, an urgent need was felt by a generation of Muslims to re-evaluate its religious ideas and institutions.

Allama Iqbal belonged to this generation of Muslim intellectuals. He 'perceived an attack on the dignity of Muslims as a result of the occupation and exploitation of his Indian homeland by British imperialism.'[10] But he also was not one to accept victimhood. Thereby, in his poetry, he strongly opined that 'India's Muslims were at least partially responsible for their condition due to their own passivity in the face of imperial expansion.'[11]

'Even today, the Muslim community does not value education,' Shariq told me grudgingly. 'Actually, it is all politics due to which a large majority of the community has remained backward. Which is why it was a remarkable moment for the Muslim women to come out fearlessly and break this negative image of Muslims,' he said after a brief moment of silence. 'I feel so proud today that their courage has brought so much fame to my little colony. Everywhere I go today people are talking about my colony. '*Har jagah Shaheen Bagh, Shaheen Bagh, Shaheen Bagh ho rakha hain* (Everywhere, it is only Shaheen Bagh, Shaheen Bagh, Shaheen Bagh).'

Shaheen Bagh

Shaheen Bagh is part of a large collection of Muslim-dominated neighbourhoods like Joga Bai, Batla House, Zakir Nagar and Gaffar Manzil, that came up in the shadow of the Jamia Millia Islamia which shifted to its present campus in Okhla in 1936. Collectively, it is called 'Jamia Nagar', or university town, *jamia* meaning an institution in Arabic. Before the university came up, this area located on the banks of the Yamuna, was mostly cultivated or uncultivated grasslands. Largely unconnected to the city, it was a spot where Dilliwalas went on rare occasions for recreational purposes, like a picnic.[12]

Jamia had originally taken birth at Aligarh in 1920. The spirit of nationalism was running high at that time. Among the Muslims, the anti-colonial activism of the Khilafat movement found a platform in Mahatma Gandhi's call for non-cooperation.[13] Under the direction of Gandhi to quit all educational institutions sponsored by the British, a small group of nationalist teachers and students at Aligarh Muslim University (AMU), quit their institute to set up Jamia. The idea was to establish an institute that would provide progressive, and particularly nationalist education to all kinds of students, but mainly Muslims. In 1925, the university moved out of Aligarh to Karol Bagh in New Delhi, and later in 1936 it moved to the outskirts of the city in what later became Jamia Nagar.

Ever since the university came up in the area, it increasingly began to shape up as one of the largest Muslim ghettos in Delhi. The first few residents of the area were teachers and students of Jamia. From the 1980s, though, this became the locality where Muslims from Delhi and from all over the country went in search of a safe, secure environment.[14] There is in fact a popular saying among the residents of the locality that 'people from all across the country come to Delhi, but Muslims come to Jamia Nagar'.

But there is a shade of difference between Muslims who live in Jamia Nagar and those who live in other predominantly Muslim areas of the city. Some would describe it in terms of class, while others would say that it is the intellectual elite among the Muslims who inhabit the spaces in and around Jamia Millia Islamia. For me, however, it is the political nature of this area which stood out. Of course, in the aftermath of the anti-CAA protests, the political fabric of Jamia Nagar is all too evident. However, as residents of the area reiterated, it is highly unlikely that the protests at Shaheen Bagh would emerge, had the neighbourhood not been placed in the vicinity of Jamia.

Before I get into exploring this 'political Muslim' enclave of Delhi further, it is necessary to understand the nature of relationship that the city shared with Muslims over centuries. Apart from experiencing a long history of rule by Muslim emperors, Delhi before the Independence of the country was largely built with an ethos that was heavily influenced by a Persianate and Mughal culture. At the same time, what happened to its Muslims is intimately tied up with the history of Delhi as it unfolded since the nineteenth century. Author Ghazala Jamil aptly describes Delhi as having the 'distinction of its fate being bound up in the modern age with the fate of its Muslim community.'[15] Till date, Delhi like Hyderabad, Lucknow and Bhopal, carry the reputation of representing the Muslim culture of India.

However, after Independence, as the city emptied out a large majority of its Muslim population, the remaining found themselves collecting in small enclaves or ghettoes. The first instance of segregation faced by the Delhi Muslims was back in mid-nineteenth century when the famous mutiny of 1857 took place. Following the fall of Delhi and the reconquest of the city by the British, the inhabitants of Old Delhi were driven out. In January 1858, the properties of the Muslims and those Hindus found guilty were confiscated.[16] Consequently, many Muslims were forced to leave Delhi and find refuge in the courts of Hyderabad, Jaipur and elsewhere.[17]

The next big blow to the city's Muslims was in 1947, when the Partition happened. Amidst the communal violence and bloodshed that followed, an estimated 3.3 lakh Muslims of Delhi left for Pakistan while about 5 lakh Hindus and Sikhs from West Punjab migrated to the city.[18] Then there were those who were killed or those who migrated to the refugee camps that came up in Purana Qila, Nizamuddin or Humayun's Tomb. The percentage of Delhi's Muslims is known to have dropped from 33.33 per cent in 1941 to 5.33 per cent in 1951.[19] Moreover, localities like Chandni Chowk, Khari Baoli, Karol Bagh, etc., that had a majority Muslim population suddenly changed its demographics to make space for the Punjabi Hindus and Sikhs.

Once tempers cooled down, and Muslims began returning to their homes, the government felt that for their own safety, they must be shifted to 'Muslim zones' like Pahari Imli, Pul Bangash, Sadar Bazaar. Muslims living in mixed areas were offered safety by the government if they moved to 'Muslim mohallas'.[20]

Jamil, in her work found that, while most educated Muslim families left Delhi for Pakistan, the poor labourers and artisans were left behind in the walled city.[21] Faced with the Partition violence in towns of western Uttar Pradesh, many educated Muslims from these areas migrated to Delhi. Living in the aftermath of the Partition, the Muslims in Delhi were frequently labelled as disloyal, and made to feel guilty for a historical crime in which they had no role.

By the 1970s, as the gullies of Old Delhi cramped up beyond recognition, many Muslims began migrating to either north-east Delhi, or to the vicinity of Jamia Millia Islamia. 'I found clear divisions between the businessmen and karkhana owners who moved to Seelampur, Jaffarabad followed by karigars and labourers and the educated, mostly teachers, who moved to Okhla near Jamia Millia Islamia,' observes Jamil.[22] This distinction in social composition between the residents of Jamia Nagar, and those of other predominantly Muslim areas of Delhi is visible even today. Jamia Nagar was a locality that grew under the influence of the university. Its residents in turn, were deeply shaped by the teachings and ideologies imparted by Jamia.

When Prime Minister Indira Gandhi imposed the Emergency in 1975 and a 'beautification drive' was carried out in parts of Old Delhi, many Muslim families found themselves evicted yet again. Once again, the migrants either went to North-east Delhi, or the more elite ones relocated themselves near Jamia.

Then there was 1992 and 2002, when communal riots tore through the entire country. Delhi was largely insulated from them, but the psychological impact was enormous. By then, Jamia Millia Islamia had not only anchored a new residential neighbourhood but had also produced a class of citizens trained in professions suitable in the liberalized job market.[23] There was also the fact that the areas around Jamia Millia Islamia provided security against eviction. The fact that colonies like Shaheen Bagh and Abul Fazl Enclave remained unauthorized, ensured that land prices remained low.[24] Many moved to Jamia Nagar for a safer space.

Since the 90s, Jamia Nagar became the place almost every Muslim migrant from states like UP and Bihar, particularly those from an affluent class went to, in search of a good environment (*achha mahaul*).[25] It was one such young man, Neyaz Farooquee, to whom I was introduced by a common friend. Neyaz was born in a small village in Bihar called Gopalganj. He was all of eleven when he moved to Delhi in 1997, sent here by his family who believed that the big city had better education and more opportunities to offer to a bright little boy like him.

Indeed, Neyaz grew up to graduate from Jamia with one degree in biosciences and another in journalism, that he decided to pursue, after he came across several biased news reports of the Batla House encounter that had taken place a few steps away from where he lived in Jamia Nagar.

After graduating, Neyaz worked with a leading national daily. A few years back, he published a memoir titled, *An Ordinary Man's Guide to Rising Radicalism: Growing Up Muslim in India.* It is a rich, detailed account of what it meant to grow up as a Muslim in the post-liberalized India of 1990s and 2000s. Neyaz begins the book with an account of a 2008 incident wherein a couple of boys living in Batla House, were shot dead in a police encounter in connection with a string of bomb blasts that had rocked the capital in September of that year. The encounter also led to multiple arrests of local people. The incident had caused a huge uproar. Politicians, activists, students and teachers of Jamia carried out protests against what they believed was a fake encounter. Consequently, the Delhi High Court had directed the National Human Rights Commission to prepare a detailed report. Based on that report, a year later, the court cleared the police of any wrongdoing. Years later, however, Batla House continues to haunt the residents of this 'safe, cosy neighbourhood'.[26]

Neyaz pens down evocatively his reaction to the news of those two young boys being gunned down, and the psychological impact it had on him, a 22-year-old student at Jamia at that time. 'I remember thinking that they sounded rather like me. It was so close that it scared me. It was as if they were me—only the names were different,' he writes, paranoia dripping from every word.[27] At another point in the same chapter, he recognizes the reader scoffing at his paranoia as he writes: 'If that sounds paranoid to you, you can thank your stars you were not born into a Muslim family. Or you too might know what we went through all those days in the ghetto of—what many call—Pakistanis.'

I wanted to meet Neyaz to understand what it meant for an ambitious young man like him to be living in Delhi, in one of its 'Muslim enclaves' with a 'Muslim' name. Neyaz is vocal about his religious identity. But he is far from being religious. If his memoir is any reflection of the person that he is, then he would be any other young professional in the city, working in a corporate space, concerned about salary hikes and job opportunities. He is really the archetype of the young Jamia Nagar resident.

He met me at a small restaurant, known by the name Zahra, located a few steps from the University. We sat over a cup of Tandoori chai, apparently a speciality of the place. Neyaz looked young, much younger than what I thought him to be when I spoke to him over the phone a week back. Perhaps it was the depth of his understanding of the locality he lived in, or maybe it was simply his voice, that gave him the semblance of being much older than what he was.

I opened the conversation by asking him why, when he came to Delhi all the way from Bihar, did he choose to live in a Muslim ghetto and not in any other mixed neighbourhood of the city.

'When we come from Bihar to a place like Delhi, one of the most important considerations is safety. Then if one is from a middle-class family, there is also the factor of affordability. This place is culturally similar to where I came from. Then there was another factor of a central university like Jamia being around. My cousin and many other people I knew were studying there,' he explained and then quickly added, 'There were many reasons actually. But safety and a sense of security were most important.'

'Do you not feel safe in other parts of Delhi?'

'Safety is not just about protecting oneself from physical danger. There is also the aspect of mental safety. A lot of people outside these ghettos might tell me that they don't want to rent their place to me since I am a Muslim. Or neighbours may not be comfortable with my presence. Then what is the point of living in a better locality? At least what we have here, is true for everyone. If there is no park, then that is true for everybody. If the gutter is filthy and exposed for all to see, then that is the case for everyone. So, at some point you compromise,' he said with conviction.

'But what about other Muslim dominated areas? Did you not think of living in Seelampur, Jaffrabad or perhaps parts of Old Delhi?'

'There are not many places which will have an institution like Jamia in its vicinity. Call it our class bias. So, among the Muslims, the lower class or those working in factories would go to places like Seelampur or Jaffrabad. I have different aspirations. They are more academic. I would like to take a formal sector job. So, it helps to have a university and a certain kind of people in the neighbourhood. This neighbourhood is very different from other Muslim areas of Delhi,' Neyaz explained.

'It is not that everyone here is middle or upper-middle class. There are factory workers also. But there are a lot of people like me who are in college or have gone to a college and are now working in world class corporates like Google or Facebook. What marks out this place from any other Muslim place is the presence of Jamia.'

'And what role would you say Jamia plays in building the political atmosphere of this place?'

Neyaz nodded briskly. 'You see, it is a bitter reality that in the vast arena of world history, any revolution is always led by the intellectual elite. To frame your demands or your angst, you need that elite. That elite among the Muslims are here in Jamia Nagar. They might not be in great numbers, but they are certainly more concentrated here than they are present anywhere else.'

Neyaz paused for a few seconds before continuing. 'And this elite has definitely played a role in the Muslim community's articulation of their views. For instance, the anti-CAA protests were in many ways articulated by Jamia. It started here. Even though Shaheen Bagh became the face of the protest later, its fulcrum was located in Jamia. Most importantly, the protests continued in Jamia. Had it died down there, I do not think Shaheen Bagh would have happened.'

Neyaz in his book has written about how he grew up in a religious family in Bihar, but not a bigoted one. He wrote how his grandfather taught him 'Saare Jahan se Achha' by the poet Iqbal, and how he learnt about Iqbal addressing the Hindu deity Lord Rama as *Imam-e-Hind.*

'Do you know that Shaheen Bagh is also named from Iqbal's poetry?' I asked.

Neyaz said he did not know but was curious to understand who named it and why.

'But I don't agree with everything that Iqbal says about Muslims. He was operating in a world that was a hundred years ago. Today the Muslim youth has different political ideas.' He paused for a few seconds, collecting the right words to express himself.

'Iqbal was, in many of his writings, speaking about pan-Islamism. Today's Muslim youth, especially in India, increasingly do not agree with that. A lot of people realize that pan-Islamism is fraught with dangers. It won't work, much like the idea of "*Akhand Bharat*". Any idea that considers one person or a group of people to be superior to the other is problematic.'

'Would you then say that Iqbal's "Shaheen" is not representative of today's Muslims?' I asked.

'Shaheen is not just representative of Iqbal, but of Muslim or Urdu culture. The person who named Shaheen Bagh might have been inspired by Iqbal's poetry, but Shaheen has existed in Muslim folklore and everyday conversations since time immemorial. For instance, our elders would tell us "*Gidh mat bano, shaheen bano*" (don't be a vulture, be a falcon),' Neyaz explained. 'It is such a beautiful name for a neighbourhood.'

'Would you say that a Muslim neighbourhood is always named after something evidently Muslim?' I asked, more to engage him in conversation over a name that has come to represent not just Muslims, but also the activism of Indian Muslims.

'Isn't the distinction of Urdu being for Muslim and Hindi being for Hindu a fairly recent development?' Neyaz asked me to reflect on the question. Indeed, Shaheen is neither Hindu nor Muslim. It belongs to Indian soil, where languages, religions and culture blend in with love and ease.

'But then naming something depends on one person or a group of people who establish a colony. And the culture they come from is bound to find resonance in it,' he continued, as he gulped down the last dregs of the tandoori chai. 'And when majoritarian ideas are ruling, it becomes your duty to flaunt your culture.'

'There is a word called "minority complex". This is not a Muslim thing. It is true for any minority, anywhere in the world. They feel that their culture might be wiped off and so they try a bit harder to emphasize on everything that defines their identity.'

Place names provide a most interesting insight into the relationship that the majority and the minority of any society share with each other. A 2013 report in *The Indian Express*, analysing village names in India stated that Lord Rama ranks the highest with 3,626 villages named after him in almost every part of the country, except Kerala. Lord Krishna follows closely with 3,309 villages being named after him.[28] Like Saket in my previous chapter, a majority of them must be subconscious claims to one's cultural heritage. They may not be intentional in asserting their identity. But they exist, in large numbers, as one can see.

It is in this vast ocean of unintentional majoritarian symbolism that minorities assert their culture intentionally. In these little enclaves in Delhi where Muslims have restricted themselves to, despite the many infrastructural challenges, they wear their identities most comfortably. Perhaps it is easier to eat, wear, pray, exist in whatever way one wants in a space where the majority does not exist to overwhelm the minority with their cultural assertion, however inadvertent that might be. Perhaps there is also no fear of their identities being forcefully wiped off in a little corner where the minority is the majority. It is precisely in these corners we find that for every subconscious 'Saket', there exists a conscious 'Shaheen Bagh'.

Acknowledgements

Writing about names of places is a matter of negotiating through complex territory. Names, after all, are not just those that are written down in official registers, but also those with which people have come to fondly connect. It is, therefore, not surprising that my most important sources in this book are the ordinary men and women of Delhi. The people's history of place names may or may not be the most authentic. However, they serve an essential purpose of identifying the multitude of memories and emotions that go behind establishing a name of a place.

In the course of the last two years that I spent writing this book, I have interacted with a large number of people from Delhi. I am grateful to each one of them for having opened up their hearts to me, and often offering their guidance and suggestions for the project. A majority of my interviewees are elderly people, who took the pain to sit through conversations that lasted hours at a stretch. I thank them with all my heart for having painstakingly gone through the creases of their memories and having dug out ageing documents and other objects to respond to my endless queries. Of course, for all their blessings and the unending cups of tea and coffee, I can never put my gratitude in words.

There are also a large number of academics, journalists and heritage experts who have provided me with their valuable time and guidance for this project. Following are some of the names, without whose help I would have never been able to give birth to *Delhi, in Thy Name*.

Swapna Liddle, Rachna Dikshit, Ashok Mathur, Amar Farooqui, Shahid Amin, Upinder Singh, Sikander Changezhy, Satish Sundra, Mani Shanker Aiyer, B.L. Pandit, Jai Kishori Pandit, Rahul Pandita, Paritosh Bandopadhyay, Ranajit Raychaudhury, Arun Kumar Guha, Jayanta Roy Chowdhury, Shahana Chakravarty, Ajanta Dutta, Ruma Ghosh, Mohammad Ali, Mahinder Kaushik, K.C. Rana, Reena Ramachandran, Vijay Ramachandran, Sanjeev Kohli, Shariq Ansarullah, Zahidul Haque, Neyaz Farooquee and Asad Ashraf. Special thanks to Amandeep Sandhu for going through my manuscript in detail and giving me valuable feedback.

I would also like to thank the Nehru Memorial Museum and Library, the Delhi State Archives and the Deshbandhu Chittaranjan Memorial Society Library for their invaluable service in helping me access their collections for the purpose of this book.

I wish to thank my friend Nimish Dubey, who has been ever so kind in going through each of my chapters and offering me suggestions on how to improve upon them. He has been a pillar of support and strength through this exhausting journey of writing a book. My special thanks to Akriti Sehgal, who backed me up with immense emotional support through this process.

Finally, I wish to thank my editor Saswati Bora, who was as excited about the idea for this book as I was when I first approached her. I will forever be grateful to her for giving me the confidence to write it and guiding me at every stage of the journey.

Endnotes

Introduction

1. 'Uttar Pradesh Cabinet Approves Renaming of Allahabad to Prayagraj', *The Economic Times*, 17 October 2018, economictimes.indiatimes.com/news/politics-and-nation/uttar-pradesh-cabinet-renames-allahbad-to-prayagraj/articleshow/66234532.cms.
2 Shyamlal Yadav and Seema Chisti, 'Explained: What's in Allahabad's name', *The Indian Express*, 16 October 2018.
3 Maoz Azaryahu, 'Name-Making as Place Making', in *Naming, Identity and Tourism* edited by Luisa Caiazzo, Richard Coates and Maoz Azaryahu, Cambridge Scholars Publishing, 2020.
4 Graeme Gill, 'Changing Symbols: The Renovation of Moscow Place Names', *Russian Review*, vol. 64, no. 3, 2005, p. 482, *Crossref.* doi:10.1111/j.1467-9434.2005.00371.x.
5 Ibid. 484.
6 'How Many Streets Has This Country Named after Lenin? All the Most Popular Russian Street Names in One Infographic'. *Meduza*, 11 June 2015, meduza.io/en/galleries/2015/06/11/how-many-streets-has-this-country-named-after-lenin.

7 Serge Schmemann, 'Leningrad, Petersburg and the Great Name Debate', *New York Times,* 13 June 1991, www.nytimes.com/1991/06/13/world/leningrad-petersburg-and-the-great-name-debate.html.
8 Maoz Azaryahu, 'Street Names and Political Identity: The Case of East Berlin', *Journal of Contemporary History,* vol. 21, no. 4, 1986, p. 583.
9 Rohini Swamy, 'Vellore Now Veeloor: TN Changes Names of 1,018 Places So You Pronounce Them the Tamil Way', *The Print,* 12 June 2020, https://theprint.in/statedraft/vellore-now-veeloor-tn-changes-names-of-1018-places-so-you-pronounce-them-the-tamil-way/440184/.
10 'Day Before Ayodhya Bhoomi Pujan, Goel Defaces Babar Road Signboard', *The Indian Express,* 5 August 2020, https://indianexpress.com/article/cities/delhi/day-before-mandir-event-goel-defaces-babar-road-signboard-6539683/.
11 Philip Oltermann, 'Fugging Hell: Tired of Mockery, Austrian Village Changes Name', *The Guardian,* 26 November 2020, https://www.theguardian.com/world/2020/nov/26/fugging-hell-tired-of-mockery-austrian-village-changes-name.
12 Lata Rani, '"Pakistan" Village in India's Bihar Wants to Change Name', *Gulf News,* 18 October 2019, https://gulfnews.com/world/asia/india/pakistan-village-in-indias-bihar-wants-to-change-name-1.67227282#.
13 'Coronavirus Has Brought a Unique Problem to UP Village 'Korauna' and its Residents', *News18,* 30 March 2020, https://www.news18.com/news/buzz/coronavirus-has-brought-a-unique-problem-to-up-village-korauna-and-its-residents-2556535.html.
14 Navneet Sharma, '"Ganda" No More: 30 Villages Across India Apply to Change Their Names', *Hindustan Times,* 14 July 2016, https://www.hindustantimes.

com/nation-newspaper/ganda-no-more-30-villages-across-india-apply-to-change-their-names/story-rkQNPfJFHDV99YmCDmJ5QI.html>

15 Ajay Sura, 'Haryana Gives Nod to Rename "Ganda" Village', *The Times of India,* 5 January 2017, https://timesofindia.indiatimes.com/city/chandigarh/haryana-seeks-centres-nod-for-ratia-village-name-change/articleshow/56345089.cms.

16 Anirban Bandopadhyay, 'A Recent History of Naming' (Ep.14) [Audio Podcase Episode], In Historychatter, *Ep.Log Media,* 2 December 2020, https://www.eplog.media/historychatter/ep-14/.

17 Upinder Singh, *Ancient Delhi,* 2nd ed., Oxford University Press, 2006, p. 88.

18 Swapna Liddle, *Connaught Place and the Making of New Delhi,* Speaking Tiger, 2018, p. 56.

19 Narayani Gupta, 'Delhi's History as Reflected in Its Toponomy', *Celebrating Delhi,* edited by Mala Dayal, Penguin (Penguin and RH hadn't imerged in 2010) India, 2010, pp. 115–35.

20 Sunil Kumar, *The Present in Delhi`s Past,* Three Essays Collectives, 2010, p. 125.

21 Valay Singh, *Ayodhya: City of Faith, City of Discord,* Aleph Book Company, 2018.

Chandni Chowk

1 Swapna Liddle, *Chandni Chowk: The Mughal City of Old Delhi,* Speaking Tiger, 2017.

2. Stephen Blake, *Shahjahanabad: The Sovereign City in Mughal India 1639–1739 (Cambridge South Asian Studies),* Cambridge University Press, 2002, p. 27.

3. Inayat Khan, et al. *The Shah Jahan Nama of Inayat Khan,*

Oxford University Press, 1990, p. 406.

4. Stephen Blake, *Shahjahanabad: The Sovereign City in Mughal India 1639–1739 (Cambridge South Asian Studies)*, Cambridge University Press, 2002, p. 28.
5. Ibid. 28.
6. Swapna Liddle, *Chandni Chowk: The Mughal City of Old Delhi*, Speaking Tiger, 2017.
7. Stephen Blake, *Shahjahanabad: The Sovereign City in Mughal India 1639–1739 (Cambridge South Asian Studies)*, Cambridge University Press, 2002, p. 32.
8. Swapna Liddle, *Chandni Chowk: The Mughal City of Old Delhi*, Speaking Tiger, 2017, p. 451, 'Liddle has noted the observation made by the Venetian writer Niccolai Manucci who described the women's bazaar or Meena Bazaar being held inside the fort where the women of the fort would put up stalls selling handicrafts, fabrics, jewels among other things.'
9. Ibid. 257.
10. Ibid. 1336.
11. R.V. Smith, 'Kuchas and Katras Keep Their Tales', *The Hindu*, 26 October 2015, https://www.thehindu.com/features/metroplus/society/kuchas-and-katras-keep-their-tales/article7800505.ece.
12. Ira Mukhoty, *Daughters of the Sun: Empresses, Queens and Begums of the Mughal Empire*, Aleph Book Company, 2018, p. 128.
13. Ibid. 128.
14. Ibid. 139.
15. Swapna Liddle, *Chandni Chowk: The Mughal City of Old Delhi*, Speaking Tiger, 2017, p. 264.
16. Niccolao Manucci, *Storia Do Mogor*, Vol. 1, *J. Murray*, 1907, p. 216.

17. Francois Bernier, *Travels in the Mogul Empire. A.D. 1656–1668*, Munshiram Manoharlal Publishers Pvt Ltd, 1992, p. 11.
18. Ira Mukhoty, *Daughters of the Sun: Empresses, Queens and Begums of the Mughal Empire*, Aleph Book Company, 2018, p. 194.
19. Stephen Blake, *Shahjahanabad: The Sovereign City in Mughal India 1639–1739 (Cambridge South Asian Studies)*, Cambridge University Press, 2002, p. 55.
20. Ira Mukhoty, *Daughters of the Sun: Empresses, Queens and Begums of the Mughal Empire*, Aleph Book Company, 2018, p. 140.
21. Stephen Blake, *Shahjahanabad: The Sovereign City in Mughal India 1639–1739 (Cambridge South Asian Studies)*, Cambridge University Press, 2002, p. 56
22. Ibid. 55.
23. Ibid. 56.
24. Swapna Liddle, *Chandni Chowk: The Mughal City of Old Delhi*, Speaking Tiger, 2017, p. 1368.
25. 'Yogi Govt Renames Faizabad District as Ayodhya, Gets Everyone Talking Online', *The Indian Express*, 6 November 2018, indianexpress.com/article/trending/trending-in-india/uttar-pradesh-govt-renames-faizabad-as-ayodhya-gets-everyone-talking-online-5436337.
26. 'Uttar Pradesh Cabinet Approves Renaming of Allahabad to Prayagraj', *The Economic Times*, 17 October 2018, economictimes.indiatimes.com/news/politics-and-nation/uttar-pradesh-cabinet-renames-allahbad-to-prayagraj/articleshow/66234532.cms.
27. N. Farooqi, 'Once Upon a Time in Prayag', *The Indian Express*, 28 October 2018, indianexpress.com/article/express-sunday-eye/once-upon-a-time-in-prayag-5420922/.

Endnotes

Connaught Place

1. 'Duke of Connaught Dead in England, 91; Last of Four Sons of Queen Victoria, Governor General of Canada, 1911-16 KING ORDERS MOURNING Senior Field Marshal of the British Army Had a Notable Career in Armed Forces', *The New York Times,* 17 January 1942, timesmachine. nytimes.com/timesmachine/1942/01/17/86009221. html?pageNumber=8.
2. Ibid.
3. 'Communications Relating to the H.R.H. Duke of Connaught in Lieu of the Prince of Wales', *Chief Commissioner's Records,* File no. 23A, 1920, p. 6, *Delhi State Archives.*
4. George Aston and Van John Kiste, *His Royal Highness the Duke of Connaught and Strathearn: Sir George Aston,* G.G. Harrap & Company Limited, 1929. p. 19.
5. Ibid. 19.
6. Miles Taylor, *The English Maharani,* Penguin Viking, 2018.
7. Ibid
8. 'The Duke of Edinburgh's Visit to India', *The Times of India,* 25 July 1867, p. 5.
9. Robert Grant Irving, *Indian Summer: Lutyens, Baker and Imperial Delhi,* Yale University Press, 1981, p. 124.
10. Sidhartha Roy, 'CP's Blueprint: Bath's Crescent - Hindustan Times', *Hindustan Times,* 8 August 2011, archive. is/20130103040022/http://www.hindustantimes.com/CP-s- blueprint-Bath-s-Crescent/Article1-659739.aspx.
11. Swapna Liddle, *Connaught Place and the Making of New Delhi,* Speaking Tiger Books, 2018, p. 99.
12. Sidhartha Roy, 'CP's Blueprint: Bath's Crescent - Hindustan Times', *Hindustan Times,* 8 August 2011, archive. is/20130103040022/http://www.hindustantimes.com/CP-

s-blueprint-Bath-s-Crescent/Article1-659739.aspx.

13. Manoj Sharma, 'As English as It Could Get! - Delhi', *Hindustan Times,* 1 September 2011, https://www.hindustantimes.com/delhi-news/as-english-as-it-could-get/story-eWTDagj4HGJSX91wNBJ3bK.html.
14. Ibid.
15. Sidhartha Roy, 'CP's Blueprint: Bath's Crescent - Hindustan Times', *Hindustan Times,* 8 August 2011, archive.is/20130103040022/http://www.hindustantimes.com/CP-s-blueprint-Bath-s-Crescent/Article1-659739.aspx.
16. Chitra Balasubramaniam, 'Delhi's Iconic United Coffee House Turns 75', *The Hindu,* 8 June 2018, https://www.thehindu.com/life-and-style/food/where-coffee-unites-one-and-all/article24104447.ece.
17. Ramachandra Guha, *India After Gandhi: The History of the World's Largest Democracy,* Ecco, 2008, p. 599.
18. Rohit Brijnath, 'Govt Comes under Fire over Renaming of Connaught Place', *India Today,* 15 August 1995, www.indiatoday.in/magazine/indiascope/story/19950915-govt-comes- under-fire-over-renaming-of-connaught-place-807756-1995-09-15.
19. 'Mani Shankar Aiyar Calls Narendra Modi "Neech Aadmi"', *The Economic Times,* 7 December 2017, economictimes.indiatimes.com/news/politics-and-nation/mani-shankar-aiyar-calls- narendra-modi-neech-aadmi/articleshow/61964230.cms.
20. 'Congress Suspends Mani Shankar Aiyar over "Neech" Jibe against Modi', *The Hindu,* 8 December 2017.
21. 'Rahul's Love, Mani Shankar Aiyar, Is Back: BJP', *The Economic Times,* 19 August 2018, economictimes.indiatimes.com/news/politics-and-nation/rahuls-love-mani-is-back-bjp/articleshow/65463092.cms?from=mdr.

22. Prerna Sodhi and Neha Pushkarna, 'Aiyar Mocks Hans Raj Again, Belittles Kirori Mal Too', *The Times of India*, 13 September 2011, https://timesofindia.indiatimes.com/home/education/news/aiyar-mocks-hans-raj-again-belittles-kirori-mal-too/articleshow/9962697.cms.

Chittaranjan Park

1. Narayani Gupta, 'Delhi's History as Reflected in Its Toponomy', *Celebrating Delhi* edited by Mala Dalal, Penguin Books, 2010, p. 122.
2. Sukrita Baruah, 'How Freedom Fighters Lent Name to Post-Partition Refugee Settlements', *The Indian Express*, 15 March 2019, https://indianexpress.com/article/delhi/how-freedom-fighters-lent-name-to-post-partition-refugee-settlements-5627174/.
3. Pablo Bose, 'Dilemmas of Diaspora: Partition, Refugees and the Politics of Home', *Refugees, Diasporas and Transnationalism*, Vol. 23, no. 1, 2006, p. 62.
4. Joya Chatterjee, *Bengal Divided: Hindu Communalism and Partition (1932–47)*, Cambridge University Press, 1994, p. 105.
5. Ibid. 105.
6. Pablo Bose, 'Dilemmas of Diaspora: Partition, Refugees and the Politics of Home', *Refugees, Diasporas and Transnationalism*, Vol. 23, no. 1, 2006, p. 63.
7. Somya Lakhani, 'Street Wise: Behind Names of Khanna and Meherchand Markets, A Minister Brought to India By Nehru', *The Indian Express*, 7 June 2019, https://indianexpress.com/article/cities/delhi/street-wise-behind-names-of-khanna-and-meherchand-markets-a-minister-brought-to-india-by-nehru-5768995/.

8. Pablo Bose, 'Dilemmas of Diaspora: Partition, Refugees and the Politics of Home', *Refugees, Diasporas and Transnationalism,* Vol. 23, no. 1, 2006 p. 63.
9. Joya Chatterjee, *Bengal Divided: Hindu Communalism and Partition (1932–47),* Cambridge University Press, 1994, p. 128.
10. Mahbubar Rahman and Willem van Schendel, 'I am Not a Refugee: Rethinking Partition Migration', *Modern Asian Studies,* Vol. 37, No. 3, July 2005, p. 555.
11. Joya Chatterjee, *Bengal Divided: Hindu Communalism and Partition (1932–47),* Cambridge University Press, 1994, p. 113.
12. Nitish Sengupta, *History of the Bengali Speaking People,* UBS publishers, 2001, p. 275.
13. *Purbanchal,* The official magazine of the EPDP Association
14. As informed by the official website of the Office of the United Nations High Commissioner for Human Rights, https://www.ohchr.org/en/issues/idpersons/pages/issues.aspx.
15. *Purbanchal,* The official magazine of the EPDP association
16. Somya Lakhani, 'How a 26-Year-Old Nehru Aide Gave Chanakyapuri Its Name in 1951', *The Indian Express,* 1 March 2019, https://indianexpress.com/article/cities/delhi/nehru-aide-gave-chanakyapuri-its-name-in-1951-5605771/.
17. Chittaranjan Pakrashi, *Dillir Bangali,* Sristisukh Prokashan, 2016.
18. Sidhartha Roy, 'Making Delhi Their Own, Religiously', *Hindustan Times,* 1 September 2011, https://www.hindustantimes.com/delhi/making-delhi-their-own-religiously/story-iqMtfMuus4wnya3HkqLCiP.html.
19. Chittaranjan Pakrashi, *Dillir Bangali,* Sristisukh Prokashan, 2016.

20. Ibid.
21. Perminder Singh, 'Introduction', *Celebrating Delhi* edited by Mala Dayal, Penguin Books, 2010, p. 10.

Pamposh Enclave

1. Ramachandra Guha, *India After Gandhi,* Picador, 2007, pp. 60–61.
2. Somjyoti Mridha, 'Memories of Home and Persecution': A Study of Recent Kashmiri Pandit Narratives', *The NEHU Journal,* Vol. XIII, No. 1, 2015, p. 48.
3. Jagmohan, *My Frozen Turbulence in Kashmir,* Allied Publishers, 2006. 50.
4. Ibid. 50.
5. Ibid. 52.
6. Rahul Pandita, *Our Moon Has Blood Clots: A Memoir of a Lost Home in Kashmir,* Penguin Books, 2013, p. 13.
7. Ibid. 13.
8. Somjyoti Mridha, 'Memories of Home and Persecution': A Study of Recent Kashmiri Pandit Narratives', *The NEHU Journal,* Vol. XIII, No. 1, 2015.
9. Anuradha Bhasin Jamwal, 'A Moon of Many Shades', *Economic and Political Weekly,* Vol. 28, Issue no. 17, 2013, p. 26.
10. Prayaag Akbar, 'A Partial but Important Depiction of Loss and Exile', *The Sunday Guardian,* 7 February 2013, http://www.sunday-guardian.com/bookbeat/a-partial-but-important-depiction-of-loss-and-exile.
11. Shaswati Das, 'Mehbooba Mufti, Omar Abdullah Arrested After Scrapping of Article 370', *Mint,* 05 August 2019, https://www.livemint.com/politics/news/mehbooba-mufti-omar-abdullah-arrested-after-scrapping-

of-article-370-1565015217174.html.

12. 'Kashmiri Pandits Hold Rally in the US to Support Revocation of Article 370', *The Economic Times,* 25 August 2019, https://economictimes.indiatimes.com/news/politics-and-nation/kashmiri-pandits-hold-rally-in-us-to-support-revocation-of-article-370/articleshow/70825456.cms?from=mdr.
13. Shuja-Ul-Haq, 'Kashmiri Pandit Body Demands the Restoration of Article 370', *India Today,* 27 July 2020, https://www.indiatoday.in/india/story/kashmiri-pandit-body-demands-restoration-article-370-jammu-kashmir-1704979-2020-07-27.
14. Apurva Bamezai, 'Celebrating the Article 370 Decision Is Misplaced and Vengeful: A Kashmiri Pandit Student', *The Caravan,* 30 September 2019, https://caravanmagazine.in/conflict/celebrating-kashmir-decision-misplaced.

Saket

1. Hans Bakker, 'The Rise of Ayodhya as a Place of Pilgrimage', *Indo-Iranian Journal,* Vol. 24, no.2, 1982, p. 103.
2. Ibid.
3. Valay Singh, *Ayodhya: City of Faith, City of Discord,* Aleph Book Company, 2018.
4. Valay Singh, 'New Twist: Supreme Court Accepts Buddhist Claim in Ayodhya Dispute', *The Economic Times,* 28 July 2018, https://economictimes.indiatimes.com/news/politics-and-nation/new-twist-supreme-court-accepts-buddhist-claim-in-ayodhya-dispute/articleshow/65180728.cms?from=mdr.
5. Valay Singh, *Ayodhya: City of Faith, City of Discord,* Aleph Book Company, 2018.

6. Hans Bakker, 'The Rise of Ayodhya as a Place of Pilgrimage.' *Indo-Iranian Journal,* Vol. 24, no.2, 1982, p. 104.
7. Ibid. 105.
8. Reinhard Bernbeck and Susan Pollock, 'Ayodhya, Archaeology and Identity', *Current Anthropology,* Vol. 37, No. 1, 1996, p. 140.
9. Valay Singh, *Ayodhya: City of Faith, City of Discord,* Aleph Book Company, 2018.
10. Ibid.
11. Reinhard Bernbeck and Susan Pollock, 'Ayodhya, Archaeology and Identity', *Current Anthropology,* Vol. 37, No. 1, 1996, p. 140.
12. Delhi currently has 135 urban villages. Agricultural lands from these villages were acquired to make way for expansion of the city since 1911 when the capital was transferred and more so following the Partition. Some residents lived on in the adjacent areas which were called 'lal dora', a term used by the British for the purpose of tax collection meaning red thread indicating the demarcation between agricultural land and residential areas. After Independence, some of these 'lal dora' areas were designated as 'urban villages'. Largely left off the city's plans, a majority of these urban villages have grown without much civic and infrastructural regulations, which explains their haphazard and chaotic nature.
13. Sunil Kumar, *The Present in Delhi's Past,* Three Essays Press, 2010. 55.
14. Ibid. 48.
15. Ibid. 49.
16. Ibid. 50.
17. Ibid. 53.
18. Charles Lewis and Karoki Lewis, *Delhi's Historic Villages,*

Penguin Books, 2012, p. 54.
19. Ibid. 51.
20. Lucy Peck, *Delhi: A Thousand Years of Building* (*Intach Roli Guide*), Lotus, 2005, p. 71.
21. Cynthia Talbot, *The Last Hindu Emperor: Prithviraj Chauhan and the Indian Past (1200–2000)*, Cambridge University Press, 2016, p. 73.
22. Sunil Kumar, *The Present in Delhi's Past*, Three Essays Press, 2010, p. x.
23. Cynthia Talbot, *The Last Hindu Emperor: Prithviraj Chauhan and the Indian Past (1200-2000)*, Cambridge University Press, 2016, p. 71.
24. Aditi Vatsa, 'Police Seal Khirki Masjid After "Unauthorised" Entry', *The Indian Express*, 27 June 2015, https://indianexpress.com/article/cities/delhi/police-seal-khirki-masjid-after-unauthorised-entry/.
25. Official website of the DDA
26 'DDA Allots Just 8400 Flats Because of Poor Response', *Times News Network*, 24 July 2019, https://timesofindia.indiatimes.com/city/delhi/dda-allots-just-8400-flats-because-of-poor-response/articleshow/70353347.cms.
27. Shahana Sheikh and Ben Mandelkern, 'The Delhi Development Authority: Accumulation Without Development', Centre for Policy Research, 2014, https://www.cprindia.org/research/reports/delhi-development-authority-accumulation-without-development#:~:text=The%20Delhi%20Development%20Authority%3A%20Accumulation%20without%20Development,-By%20Shahana%20Sheikh&text=This%20report%20finds%20that%20while,and%20allotting%20low%2Dincome%20housing.
28. Shinjini Ghosh, '780 Hectares Accumulated Under

Land Pooling Policy So Far: DDA', *The Hindu,* 20 June 2019, https://www.thehindu.com/news/cities/Delhi/780-hectares-accumulated-under-land-pooling-policy-so-far-dda/article28079527.ece.

29. Risha Chitlangia, 'DDA Seeks Citizens' Help to Name New Sub-Cities', *Hindustan Times,* 30 July 2019, https://www.hindustantimes.com/delhi-news/dda-seeks-citizens-help-to-name-new-sub-cities/story-pYju8y05gB0hsDH8RDDWbN.html#:~:text=The%20DDA%20will%20develop%20five,nearly%201.7%20million%20dwelling%20units.
30. Ibid.

Shaheen Bagh

1. Suparna Chaudhry, 'India's New Law May Leave Millions of Muslims Without Citizenship', *The Washington Post,* 13 December 2019, https://www.washingtonpost.com/politics/2019/12/13/indias-new-law-may-leave-millions-muslims-without-citizenship/.
2. Nehal Ahmed and Grace Raju, '"We Heard Gunfire": Jamia Students Detail Police Attack on Campus', *Al Jazeera,* 18 December 2019, https://www.aljazeera.com/news/2019/12/18/we-heard-gunfire-jamia-students-detail-police-attack-on-campus.
3. Laurent Gayer, 'Safe and Sound: Searching for a "Good Environment" in Abul Fazl Enclave, Delhi', *Muslims in Indian Cities,* edited by Laurent Gayer and Christophe Jaffrelot, Columbia University Press, 2011, p. 217.
4. Fareeha Iftikhar, 'Shaheen Bagh Living Up to Its Name, Says Man Who Christened the Colony', *Hindustan Times,* 24 January 2020, https://www.hindustantimes.com/cities/

shaheen-bagh-living-up-to-its-name-says-man-who-christened-the-colony/story-PFsIKrwerxyiEx4sCTOYHP.html.

5. Iqbal Singh Sevea, *The Political Philosophy of Muhammad Iqbal: Islam and Nationalism in Late Colonial India,* Cambridge University Press, 2012, p. 24.
6. Sir Muhammad Iqbal's 1930 Presidential Address, http://www.columbia.edu/itc/mealac/pritchett/00islamlinks/txt_iqbal_1930.html.
7. Dayne E. Nix, 'Muhammad Iqbal: Restoring Muslim Dignity Through Poetry, Philosophy and Religious Political Action', *Muhammad Iqbal: Essays on the Reconstruction of Modern Muslim Thought,* edited by H.C. Hilllier and Basit Bilal Koshul, Edinburgh University Press, 2015, p. 201.
8. Iqbal Singh Sevea, *The Political Philosophy of Muhammad Iqbal: Islam and Nationalism in Late Colonial India,* Cambridge University Press, 2012, p. 29.
9. Ibid. 3.
10. Dayne E. Nix, 'Muhammad Iqbal: Restoring Muslim Dignity through Poetry, Philosophy and Religious Political Action', *Muhammad Iqbal: Essays on the Reconstruction of Modern Muslim Thought,* by H.C. Hilllier and Basit Bilal Koshul, Edinburgh University Press, 2015, p. 201.
11. Ibid. 202.
12. Ahmed Ali, *Twilight in Delhi,* Rupa Publication, 2007, p. 43.
13. Uma Vishnu, 'Jamia Square: Why a Century-Old University Has Become Focal Point of Unrest', *Indian Express,* 22 December 2019, https://indianexpress.com/article/india/jamia-milia-islamia-university-protest-citizenship-law-police-brutality-6178794/.
14. Laurent Gayer, 'Safe and Sound: Searching for a "Good Environment" in Abul Fazl Enclave, Delhi,' in *Muslims in Indian Cities,* edited by Laurent Gayer and Christophe

Jaffrelot, Columbia University Press, 2011, p. 213.
15. Ghazala Jamil, *Accumulation by Segregation: Muslim Localities in Delhi,* Oxford University Press, 2017, p. 3.
16. Ibid. 4.
17. Ibid.
18. Atikh Rashid, 'How Muslim Ghettos Came About in Delhi', *The Indian Express,* 3 March 2020, https://indianexpress.com/article/india/muslim-ghettos-of-delhi-6297633/.
19. Ibid.
20. Vazira Fazila-Yacoobali Zamindar, *The Long Partition and the Making of South Asia: Refugees, Boundaries, Histories,* Columbia University Press, 2007, p. 29.
21. Ghazala Jamil, *Accumulation by Segregation: Muslim Localities in Delhi,* Oxford University Press, 2017, p. 6.
22. Ibid.
23. Ibid. 8.
24. Laurent Gayer, Safe and Sound: Searching for a 'Good Environment' In Abul Fazl Enclave, Delhi', *Muslims in Indian Cities,* edited by Laurent Gayer and Christophe Jaffrelot, Columbia University Press, 2011, p. 233.
25. Ibid. 216.
26. Neyaz Farooquee, *An Ordinary Man's Guide to Radicalism: Growing Up Muslim in India,* Westland Publications, 2018, p. 1.
27. Ibid.
28. Shyamlal Yadav, 'Name Game: 3,626 Villages Named After Ram, 3,309 After Krishna' *The Indian Express,* 4 July 2013, http://archive.indianexpress.com/news/name-game-3626-villages-named-after-ram-3309-after-krishna/1137491/0.

Photo Credits

This page is an extension of the copyright page.

1. Mirza Ghalib House in Delhi-Interior, Wikimedia Commons/Indrajit Das, p. vi
2. Kashmiri Houseboat Woodwork Lattice Pattern, Wikimedia Commons/Nina Garman, p. 1, p. 43, p. 79, p. 105, p. 131, p. 159
3. Chandni Chowk, Old Delhi, India - September 2014, Wikimedia Commons/ Rickard Törnblad, p. 2
4. View of Connaught Place, Wikimedia Commons/ Photo Division, Ministry of Information & Broadcasting, Government of India, p. 44
5. CR Park, Abhimanyu Chakravorty, p. 80
6. Lotus flower, Wikimedia Commons/ Hong Zhang, p. 106
7. Archways of Khirki Masjid, Wikimedia Commons/ Pankaj Purohit, p. 132
8. Close-up of wall-art graffiti at Shaheen Bagh Protests, Wikimedia Commons/ DTM, p. 160